MINDFULNESS AND ZEN COLORING BOOK

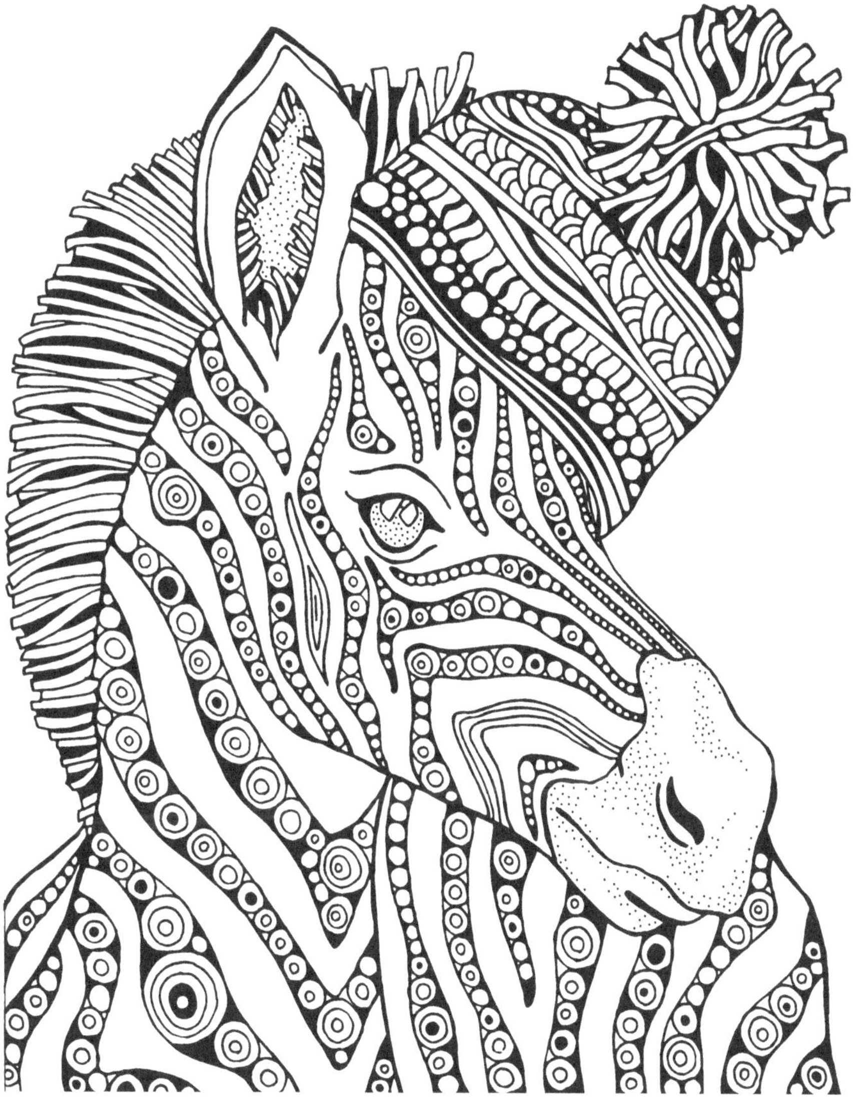

- RUSS FOCUS -

ISBN-13: 978-1727087277 ISBN-10: 1727087275
PUBLISHED BY RUSS FOCUS

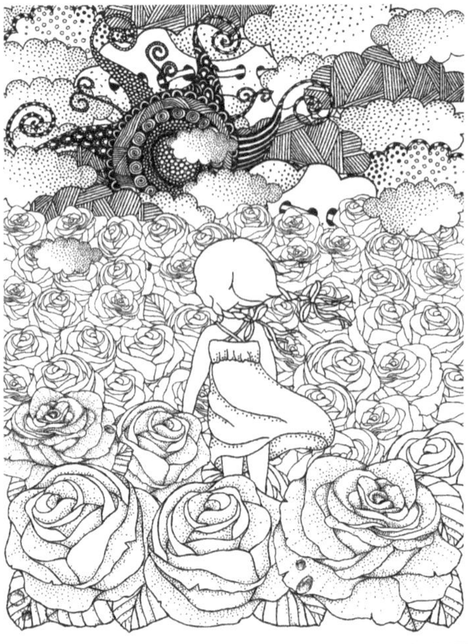

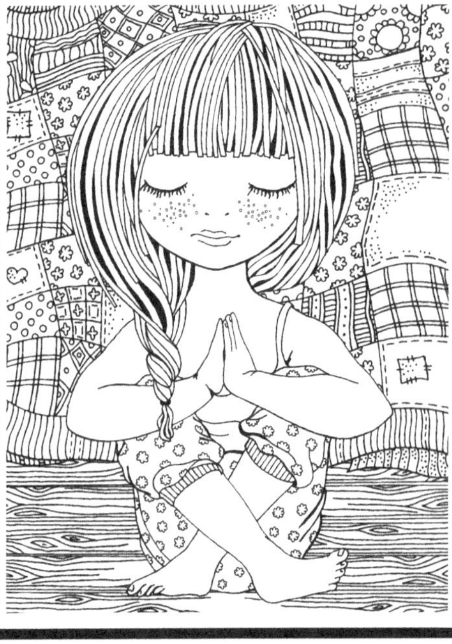

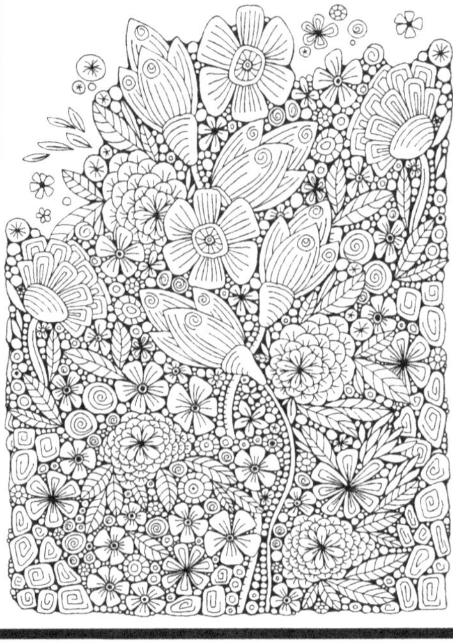

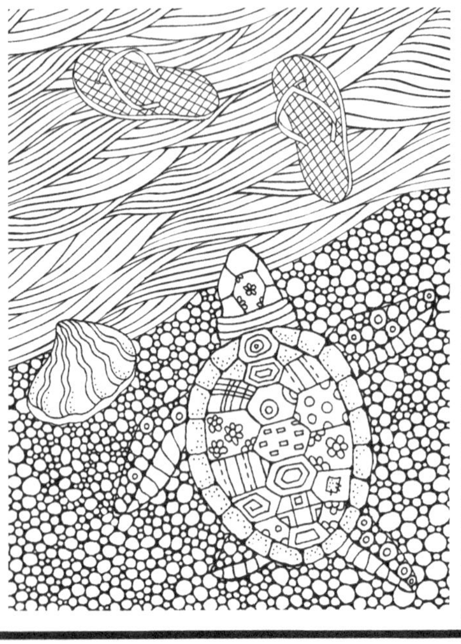

SAMPLE
ZEN
COLORING
17 of 40
PAGES

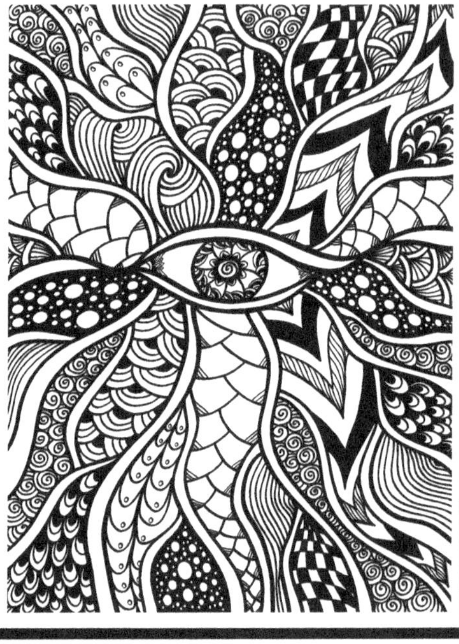

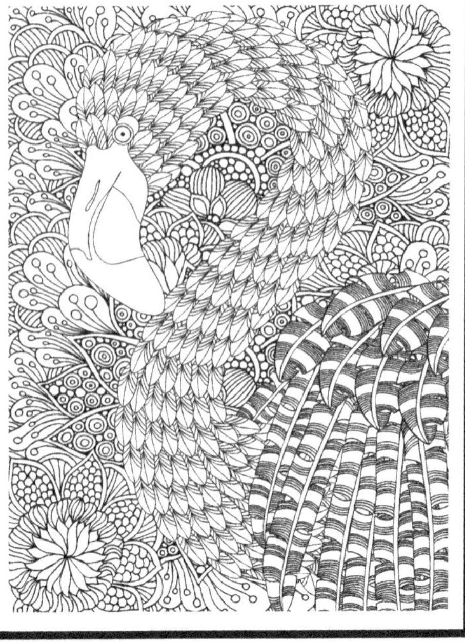

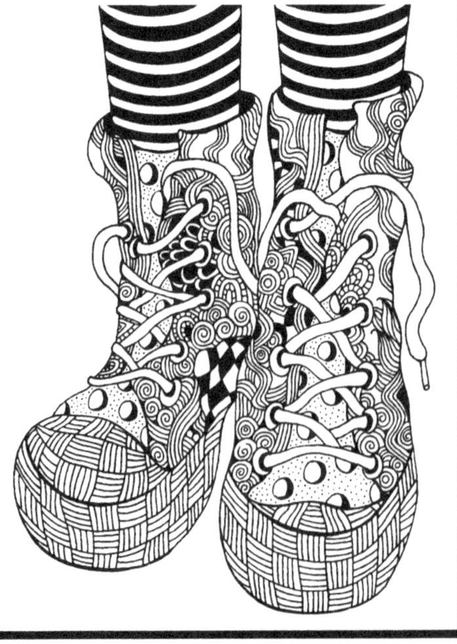

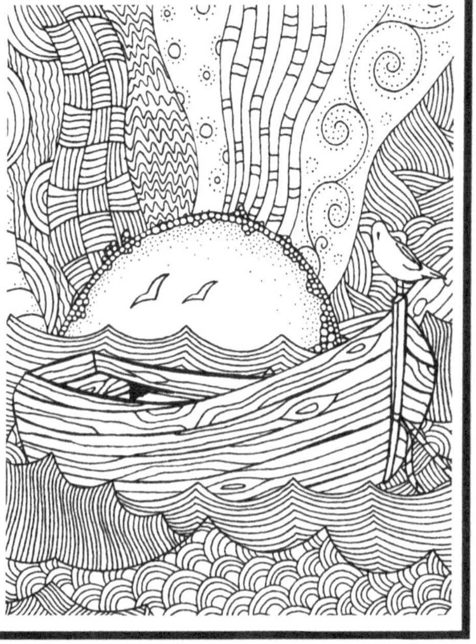

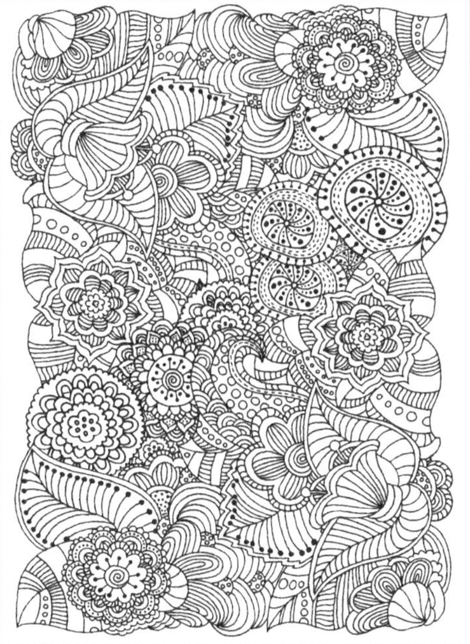
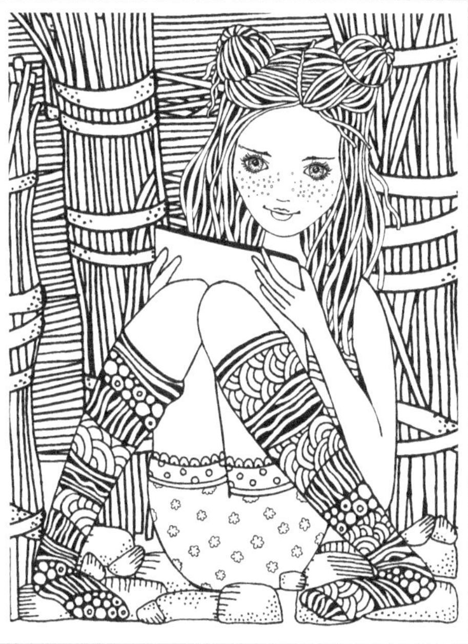
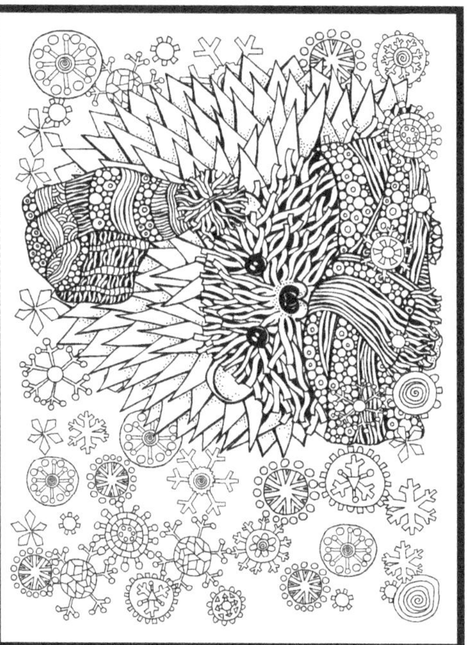
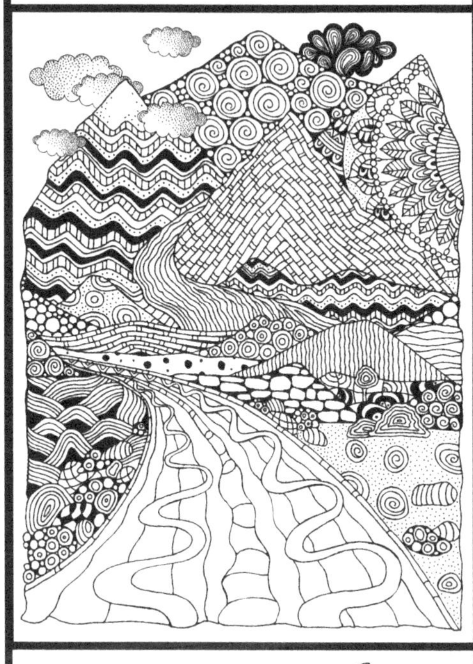
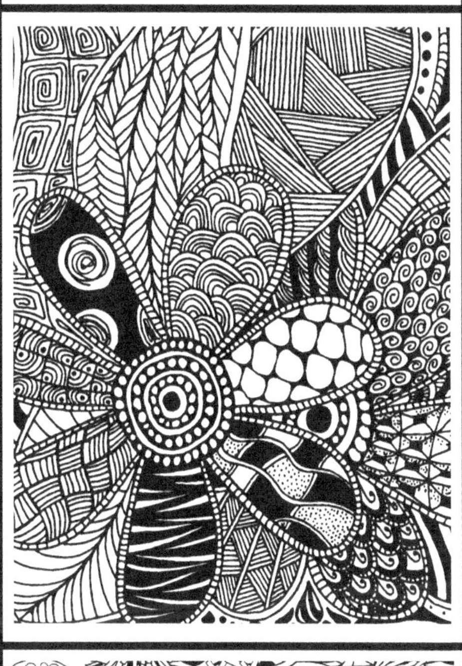
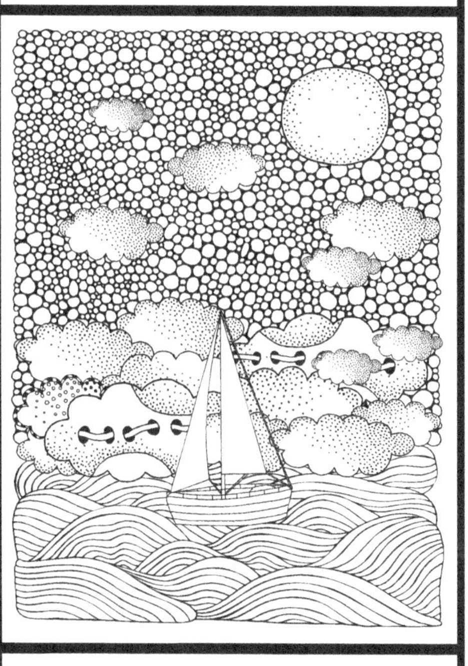
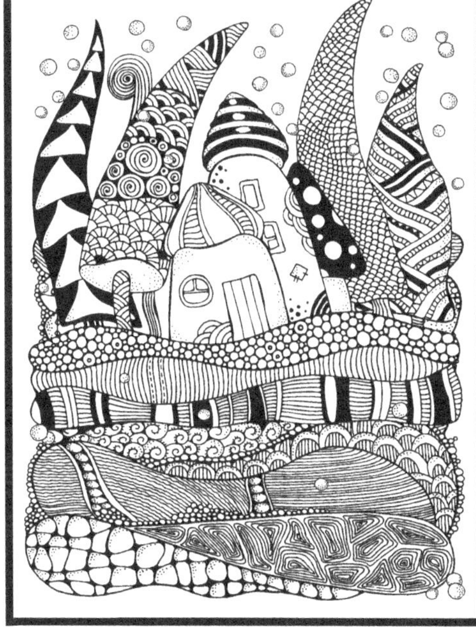
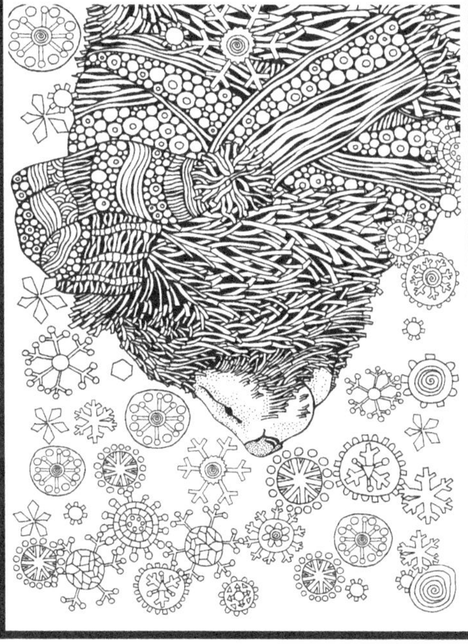
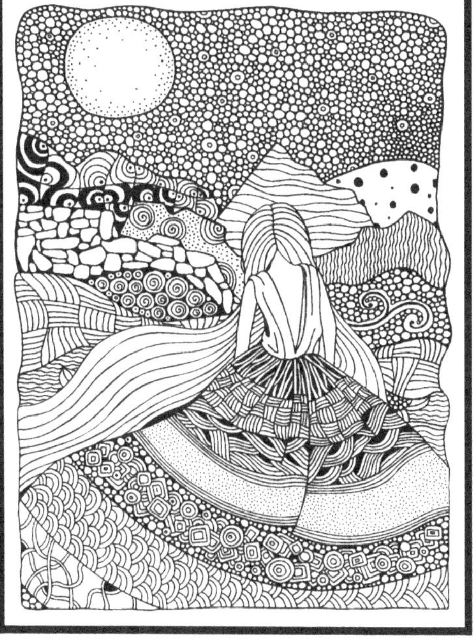

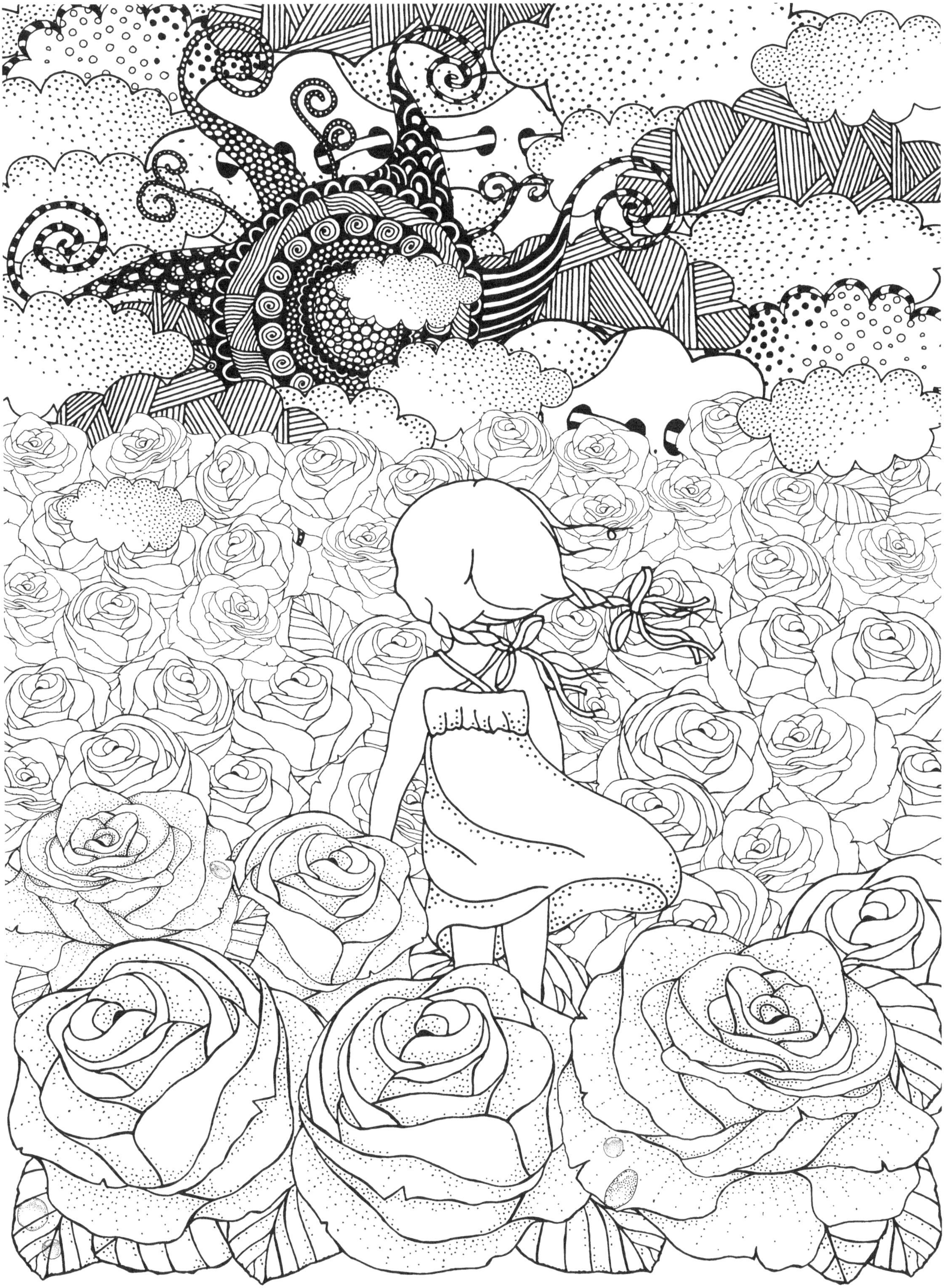

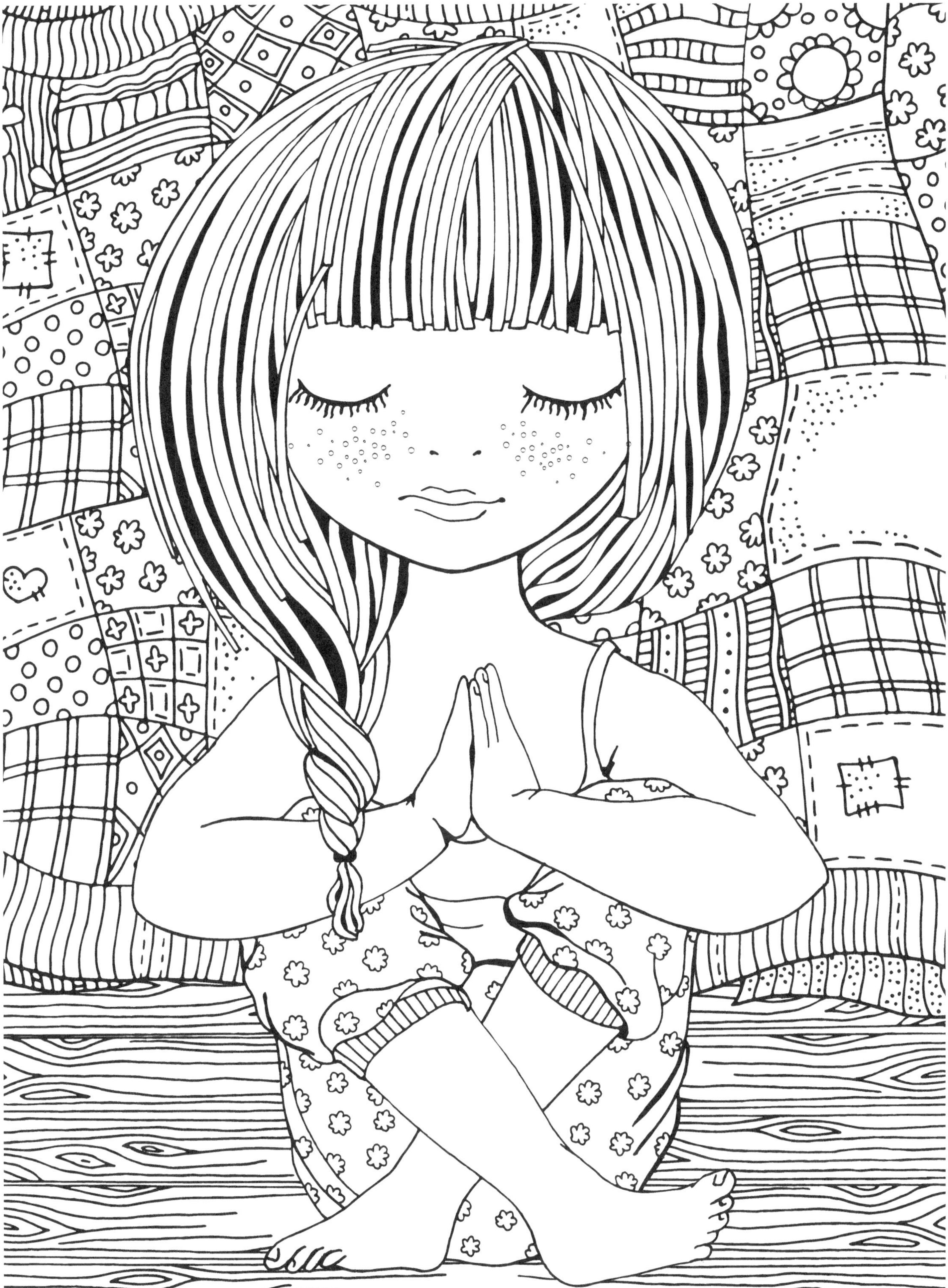

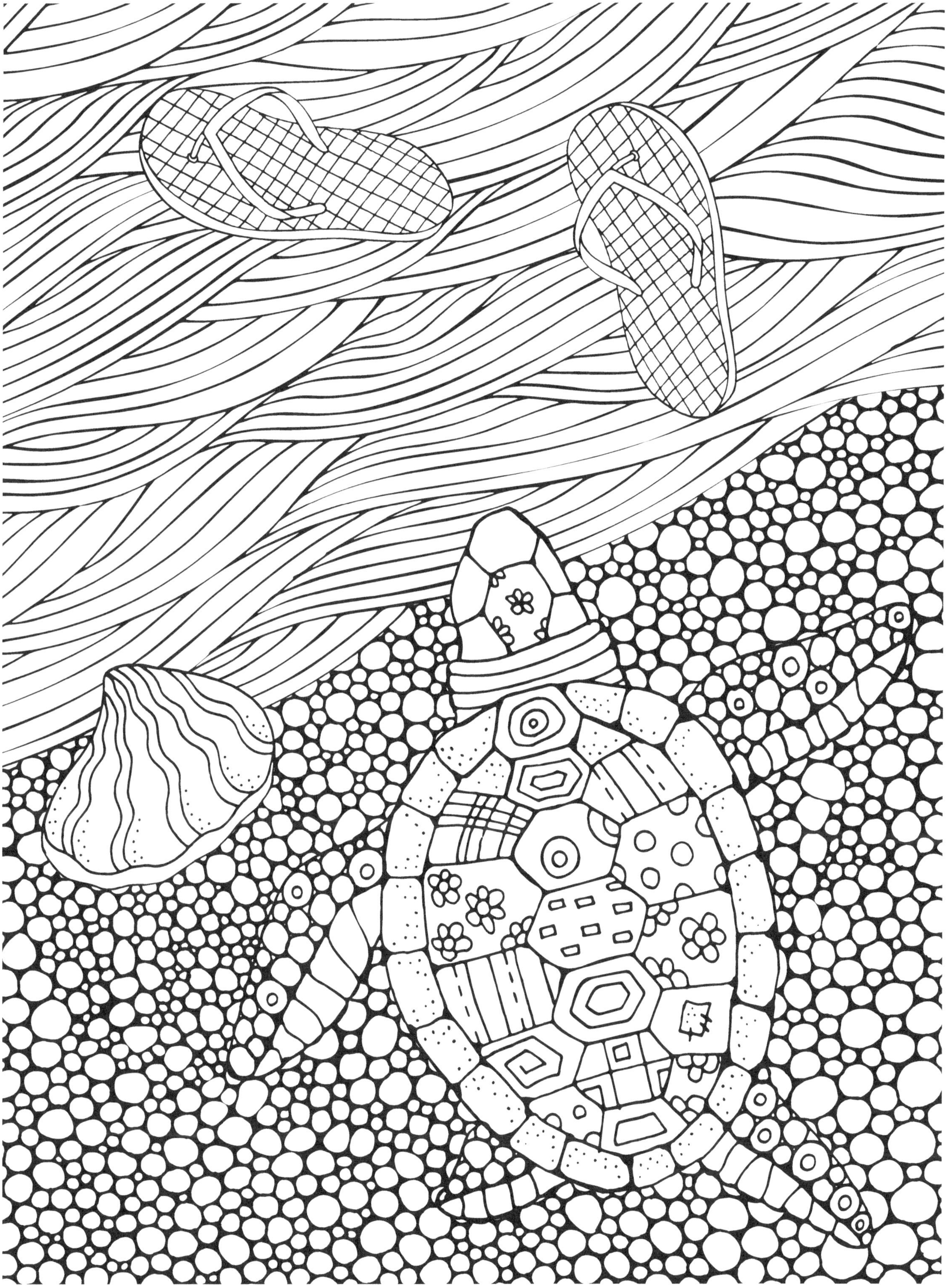

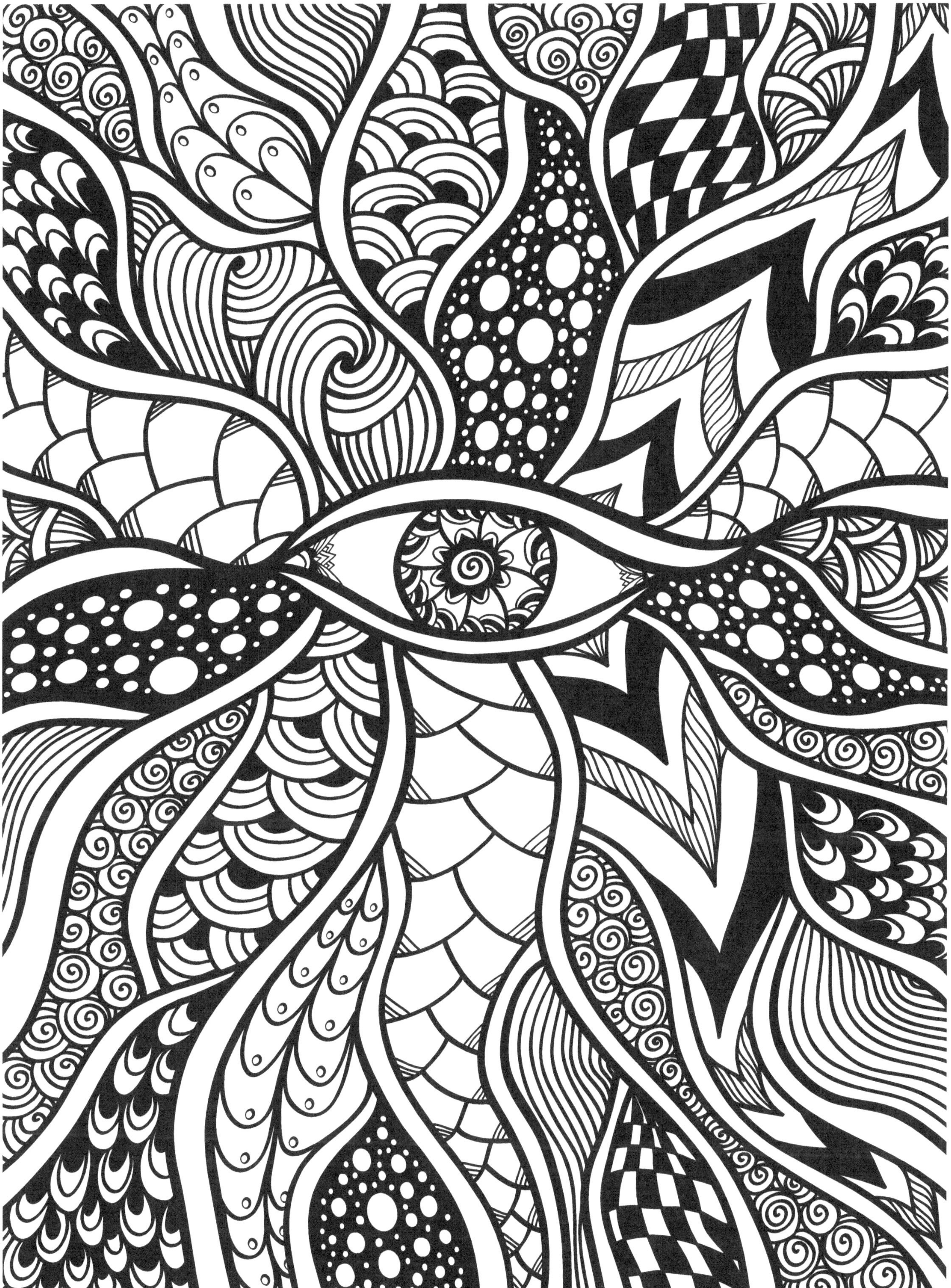

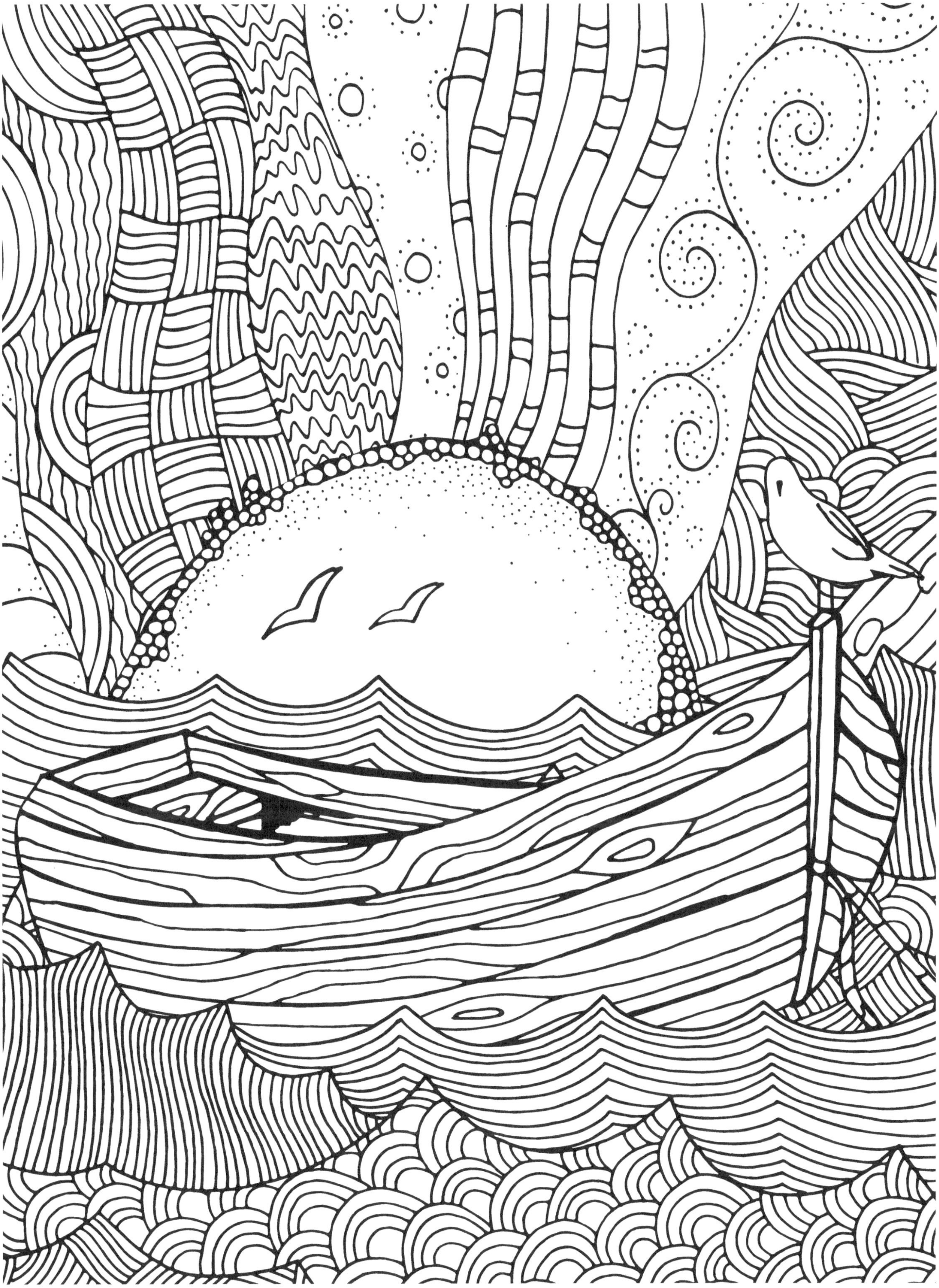

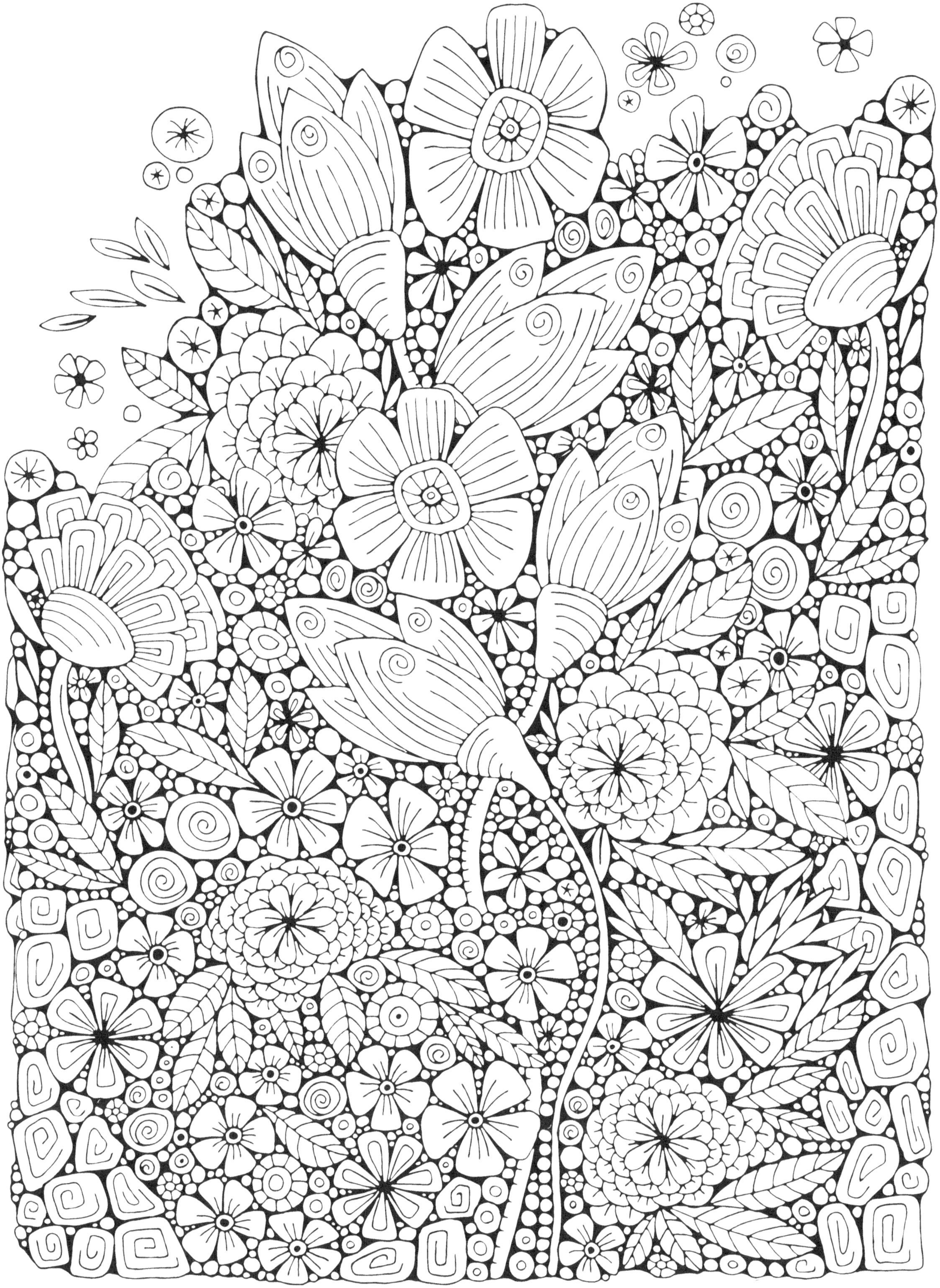

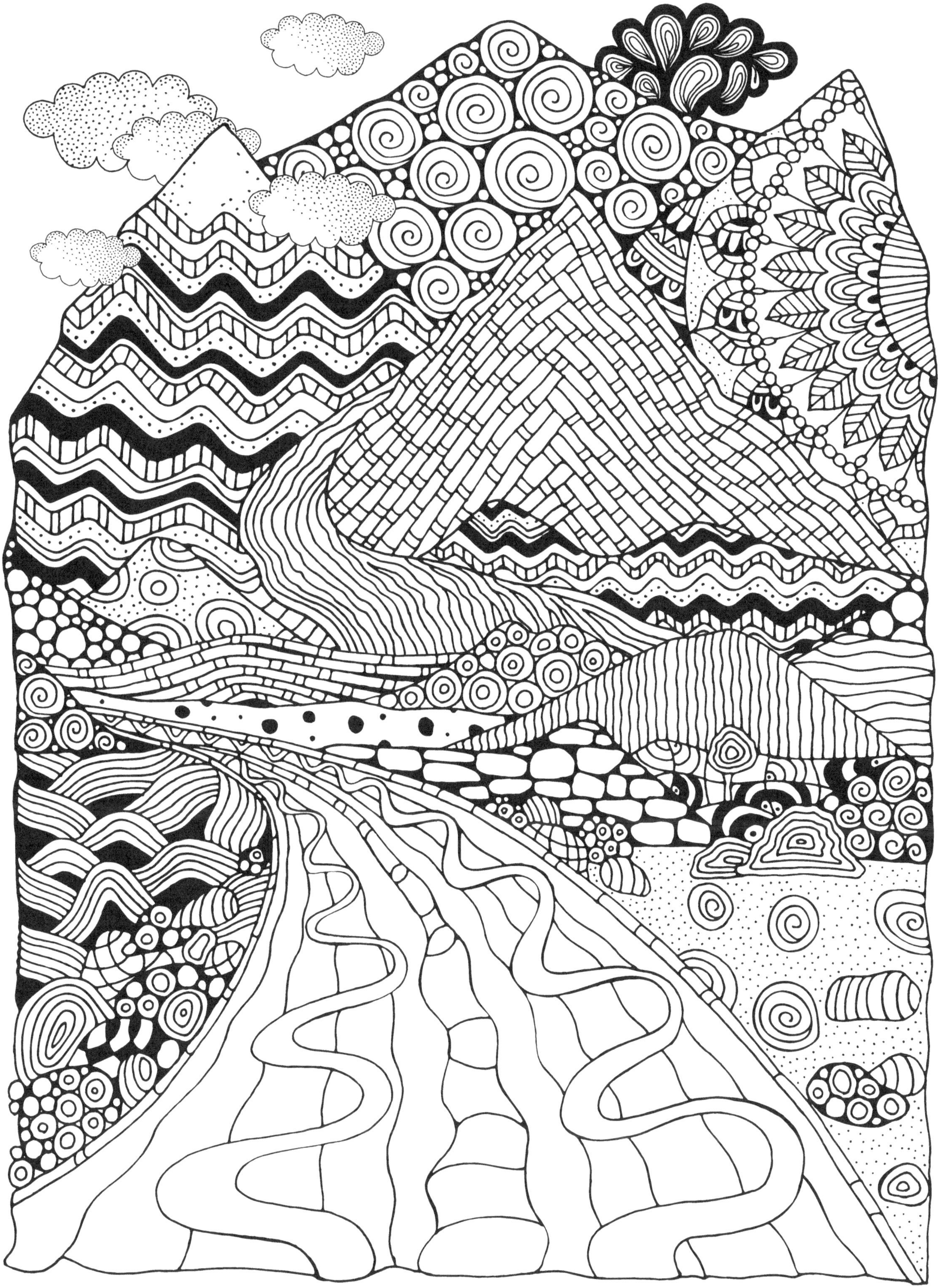

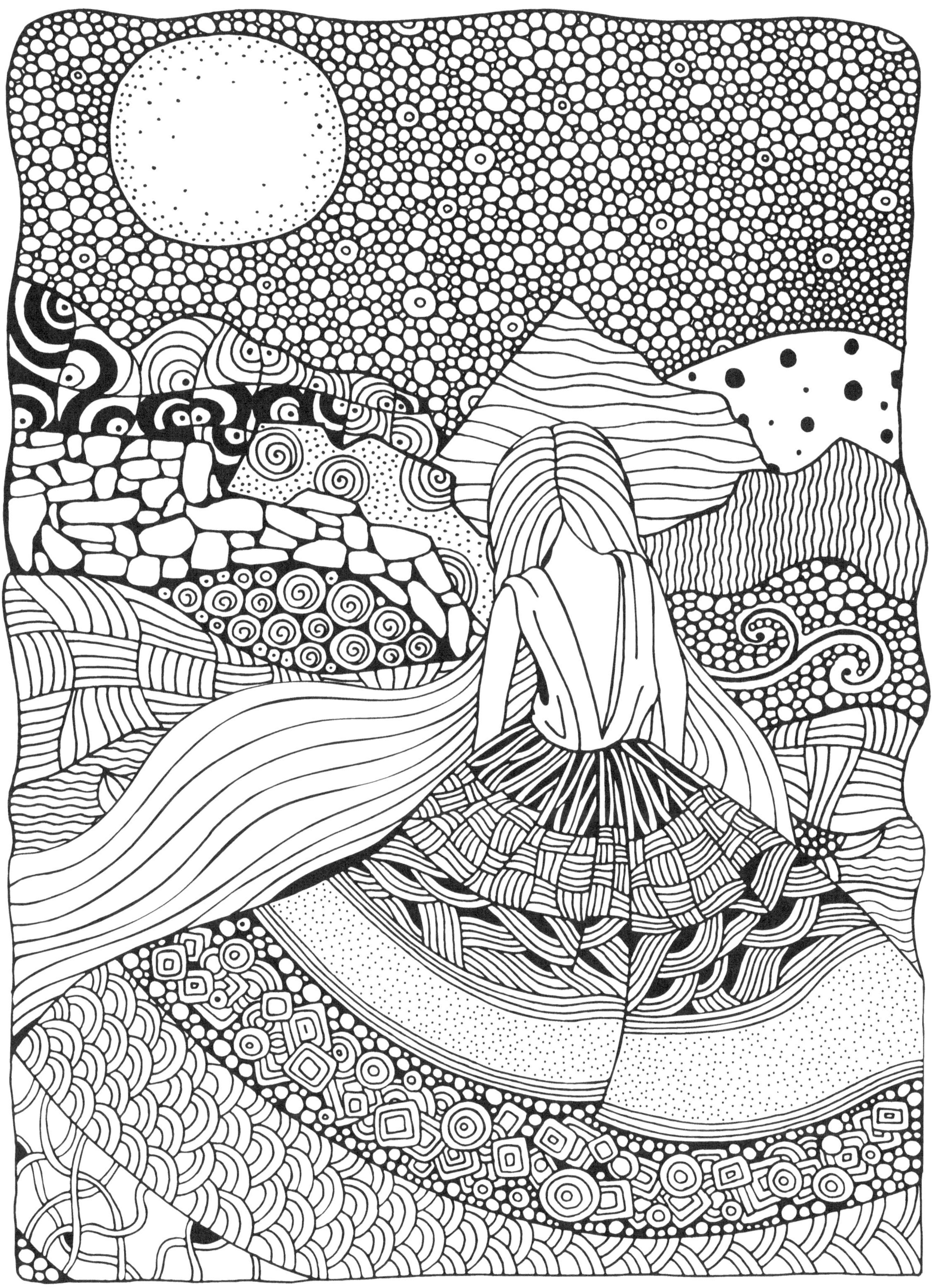

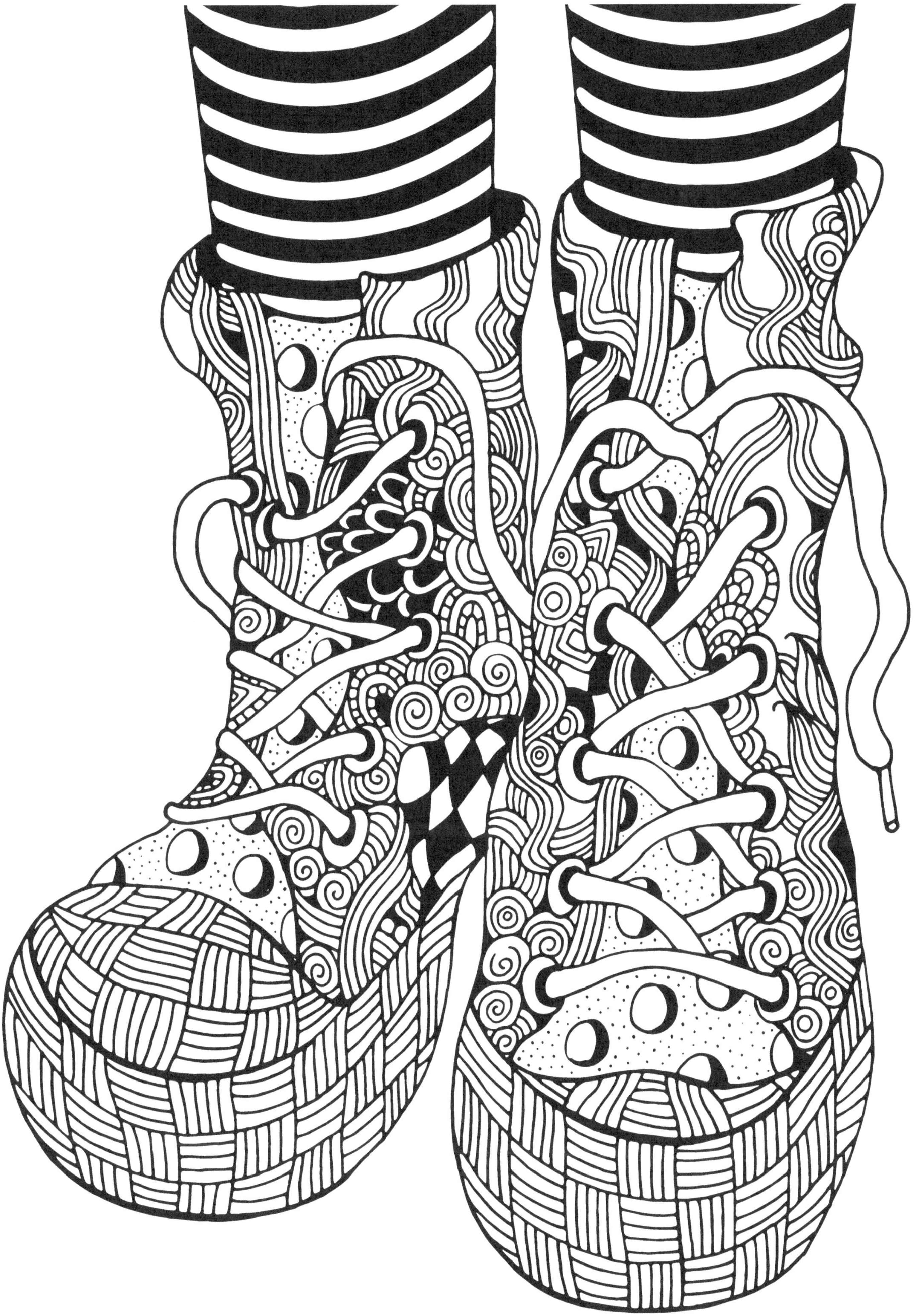

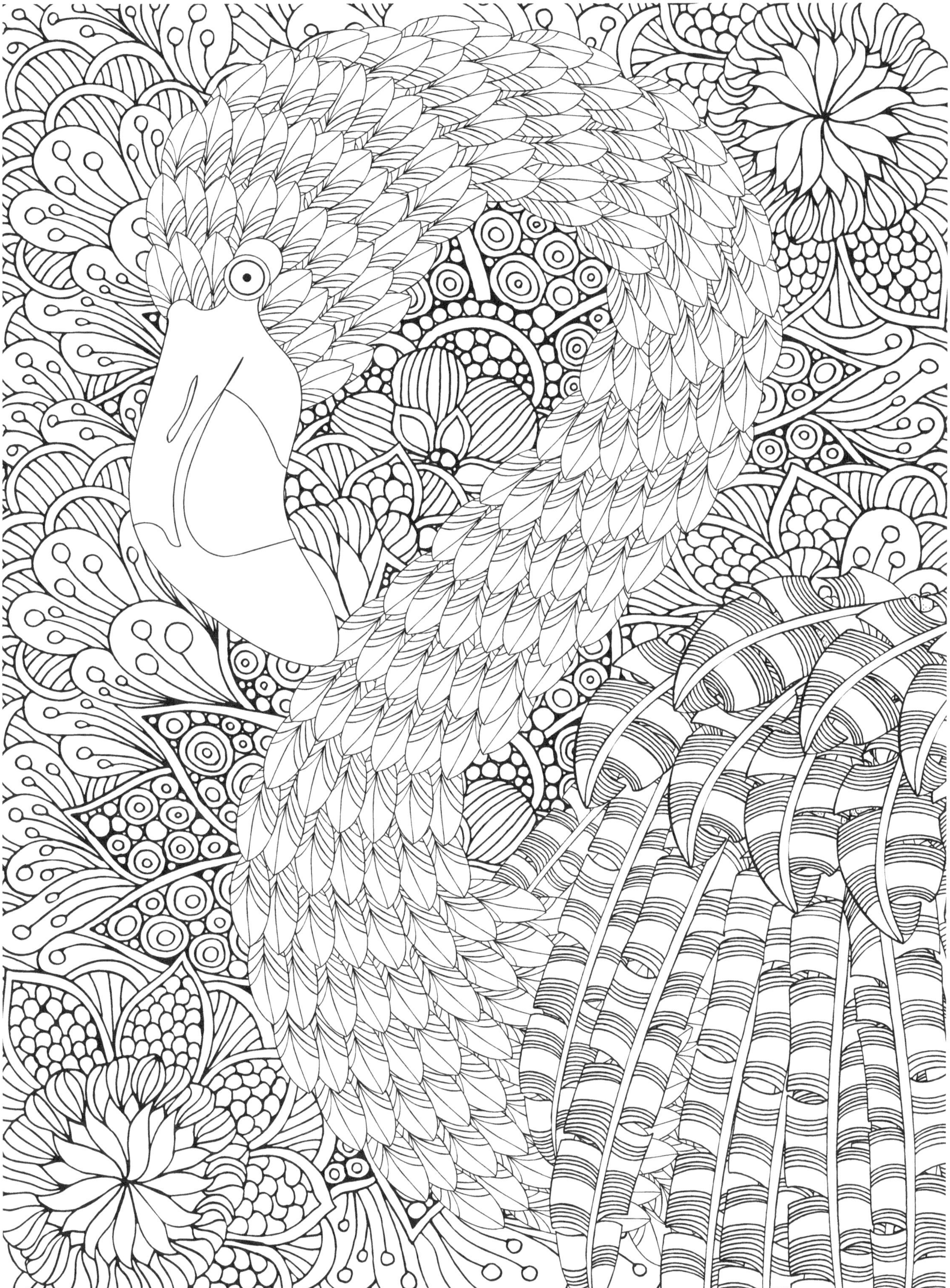

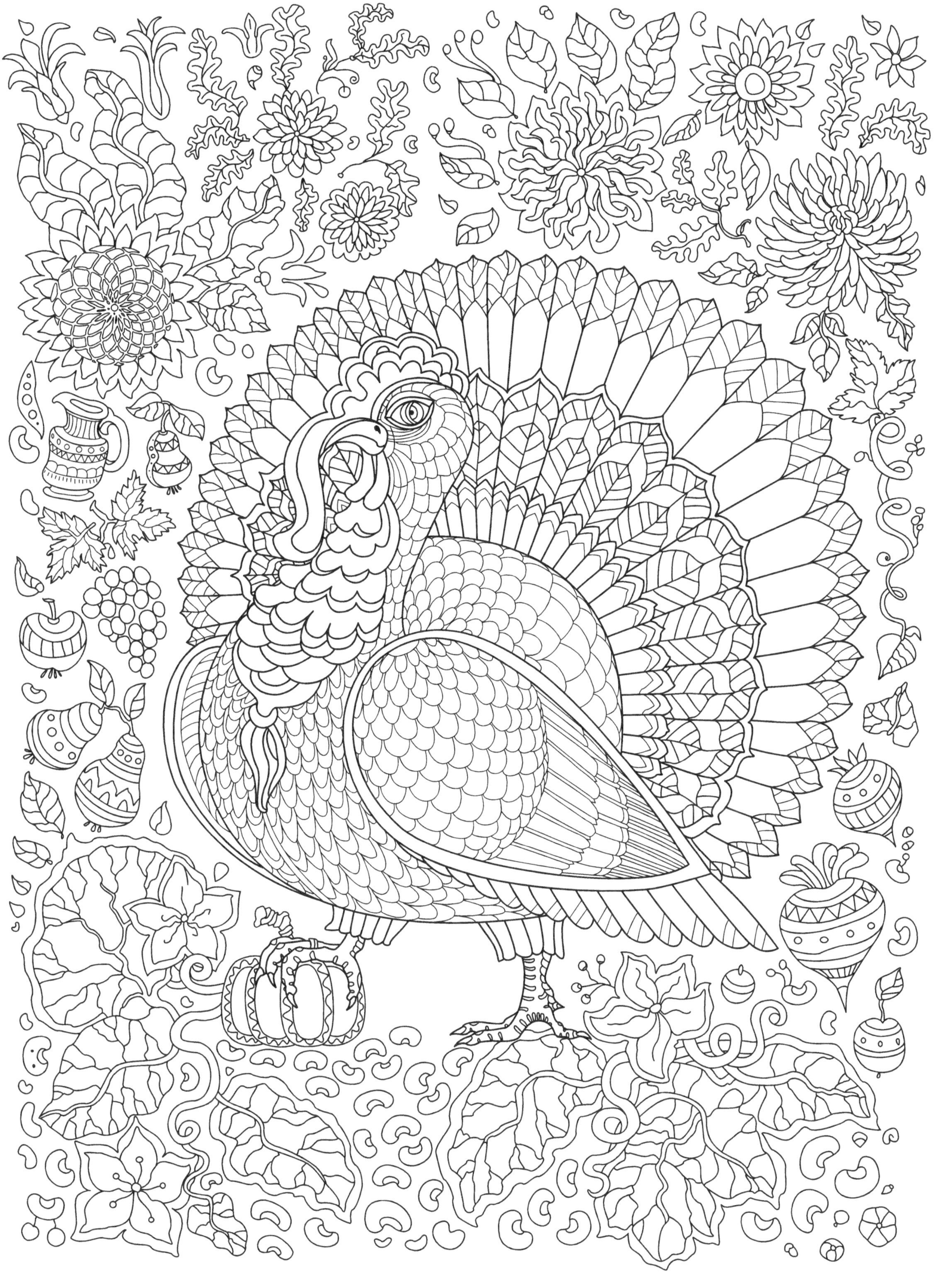

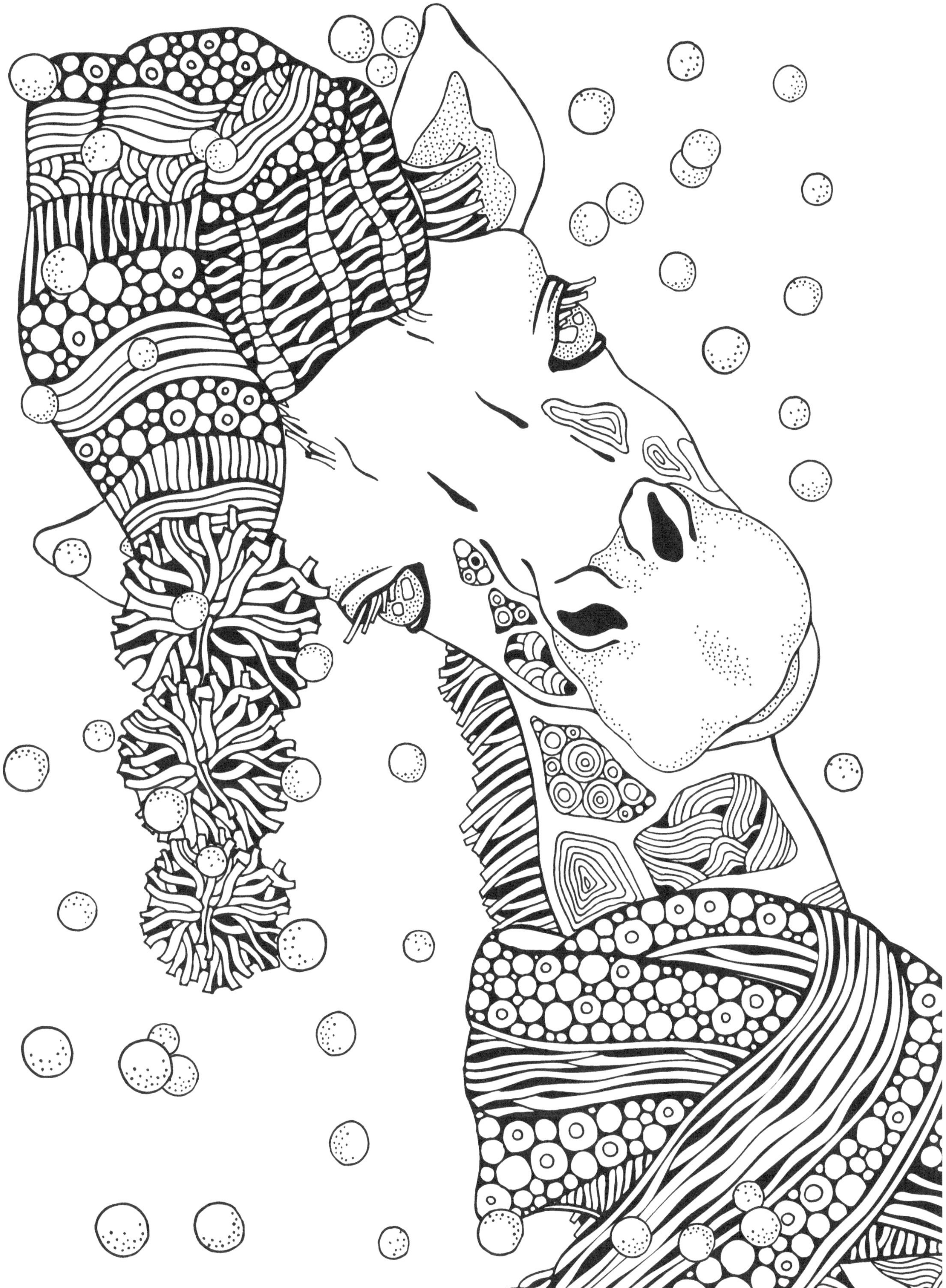

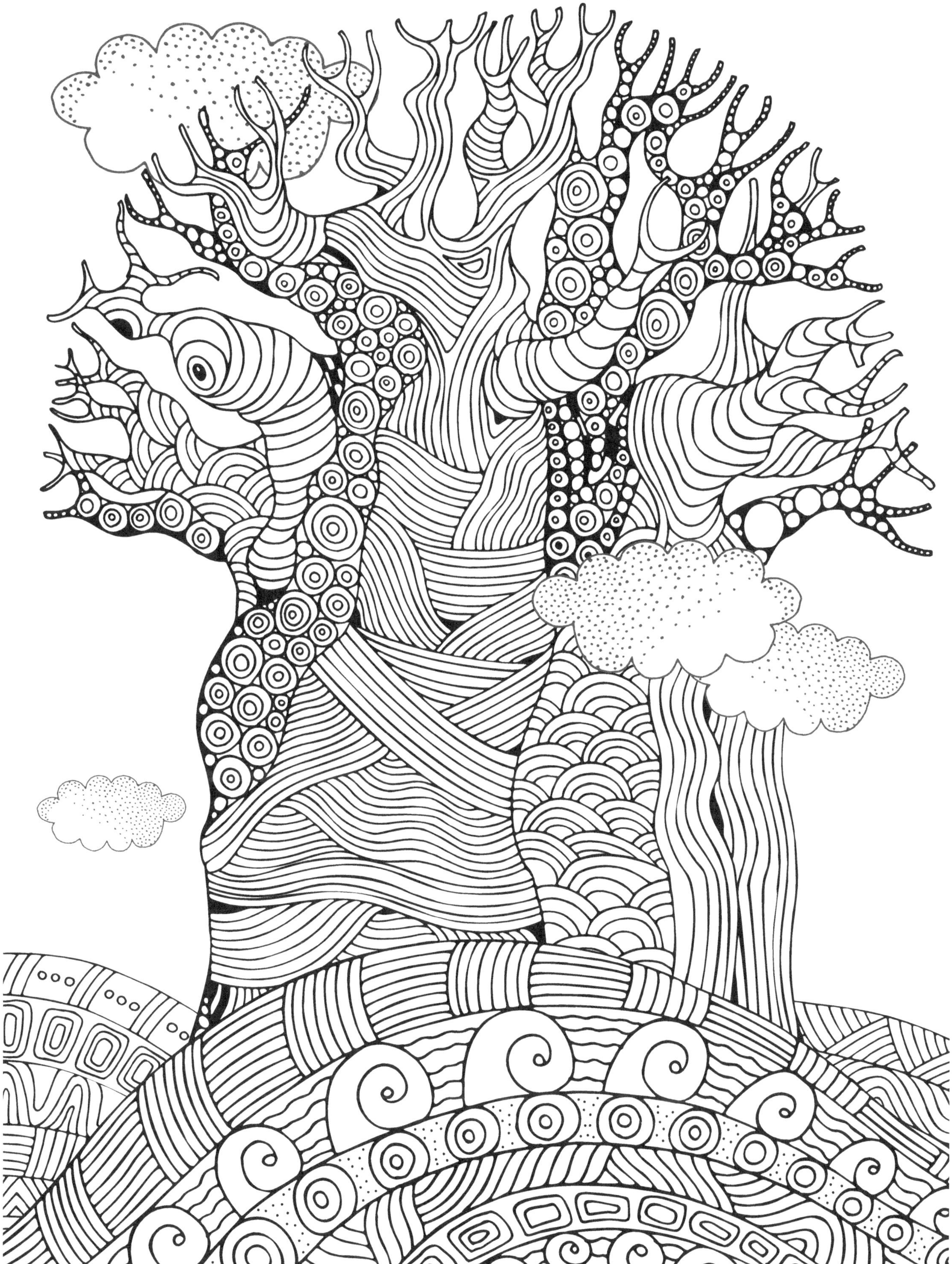

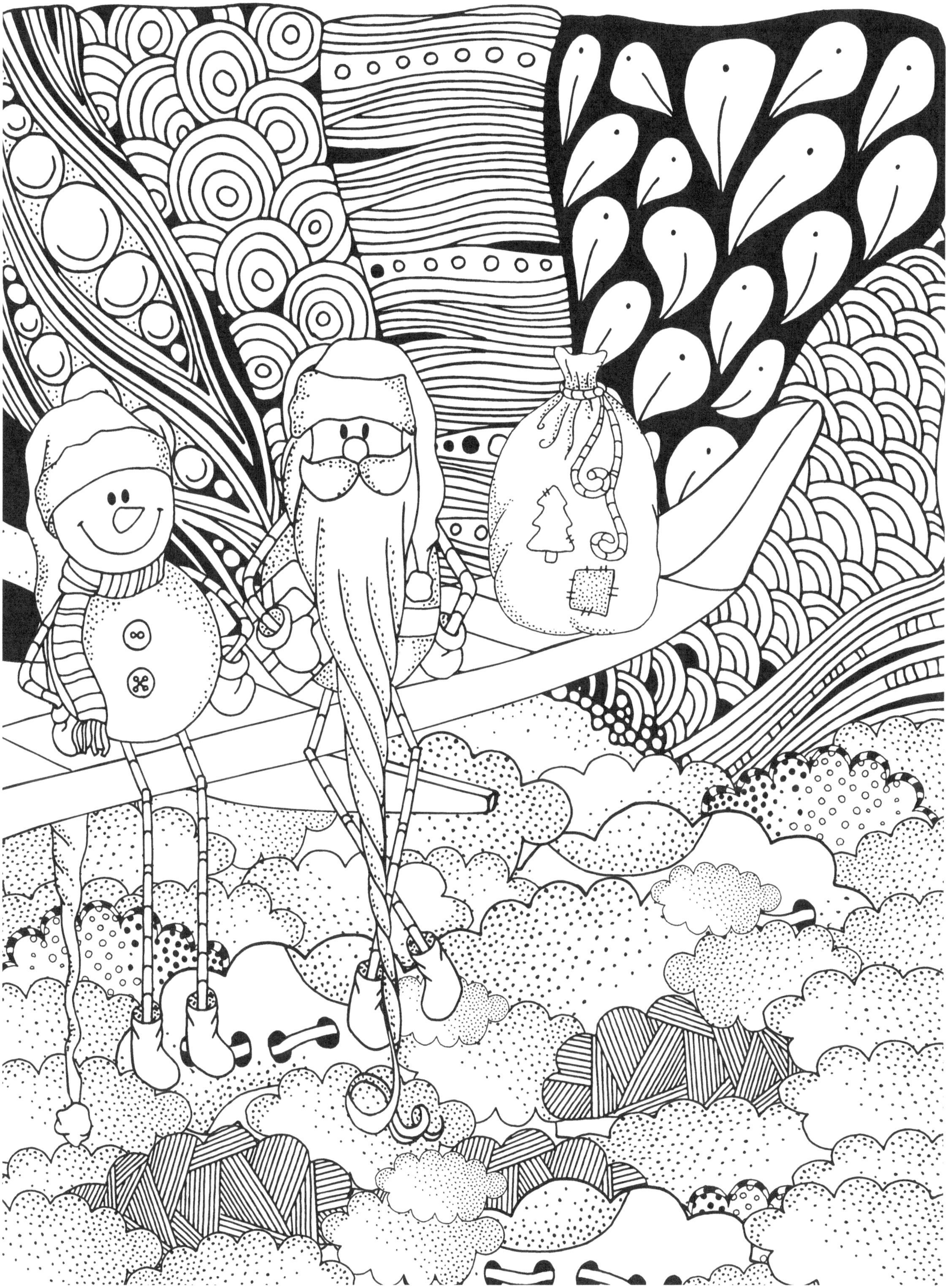

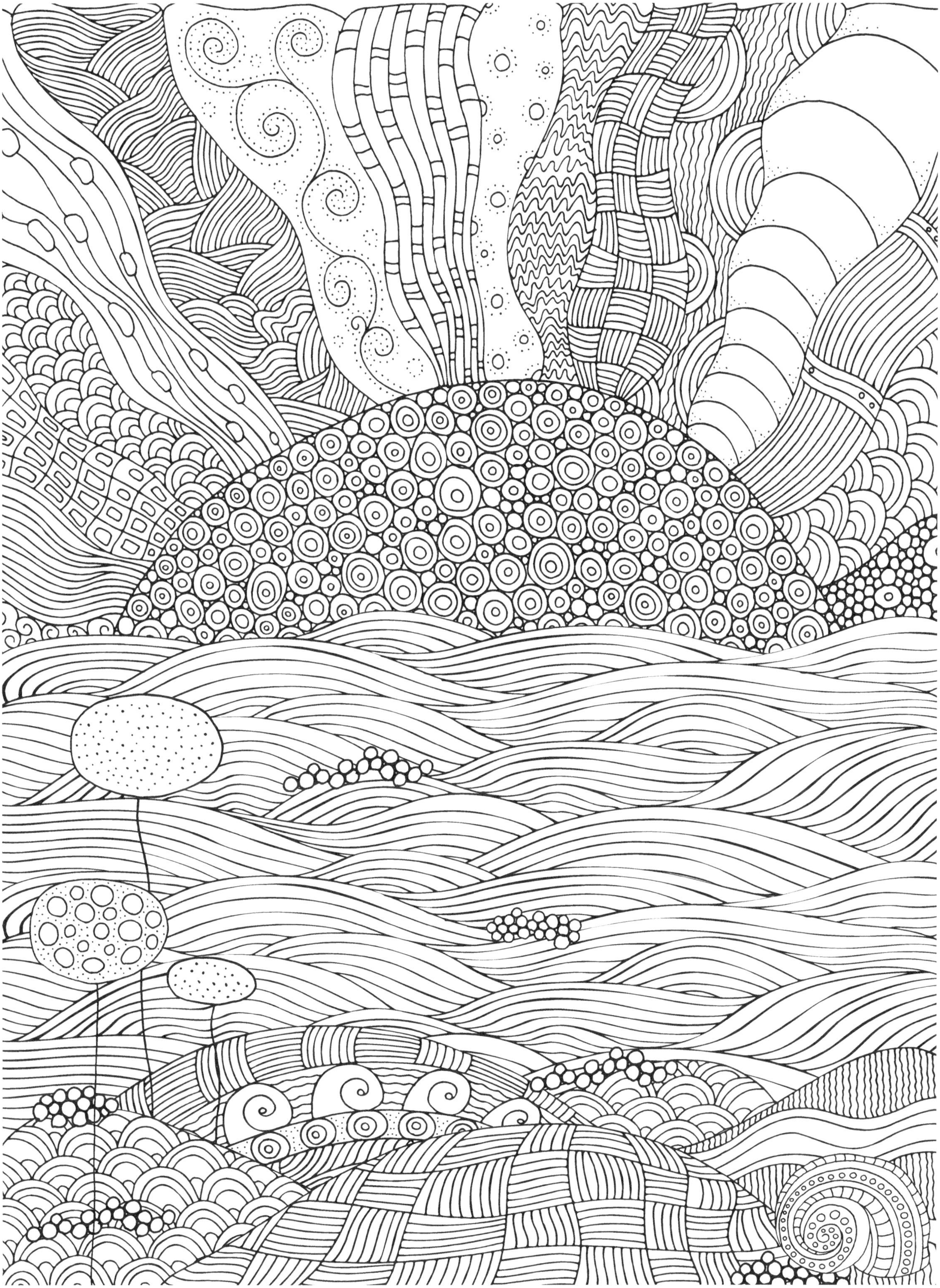

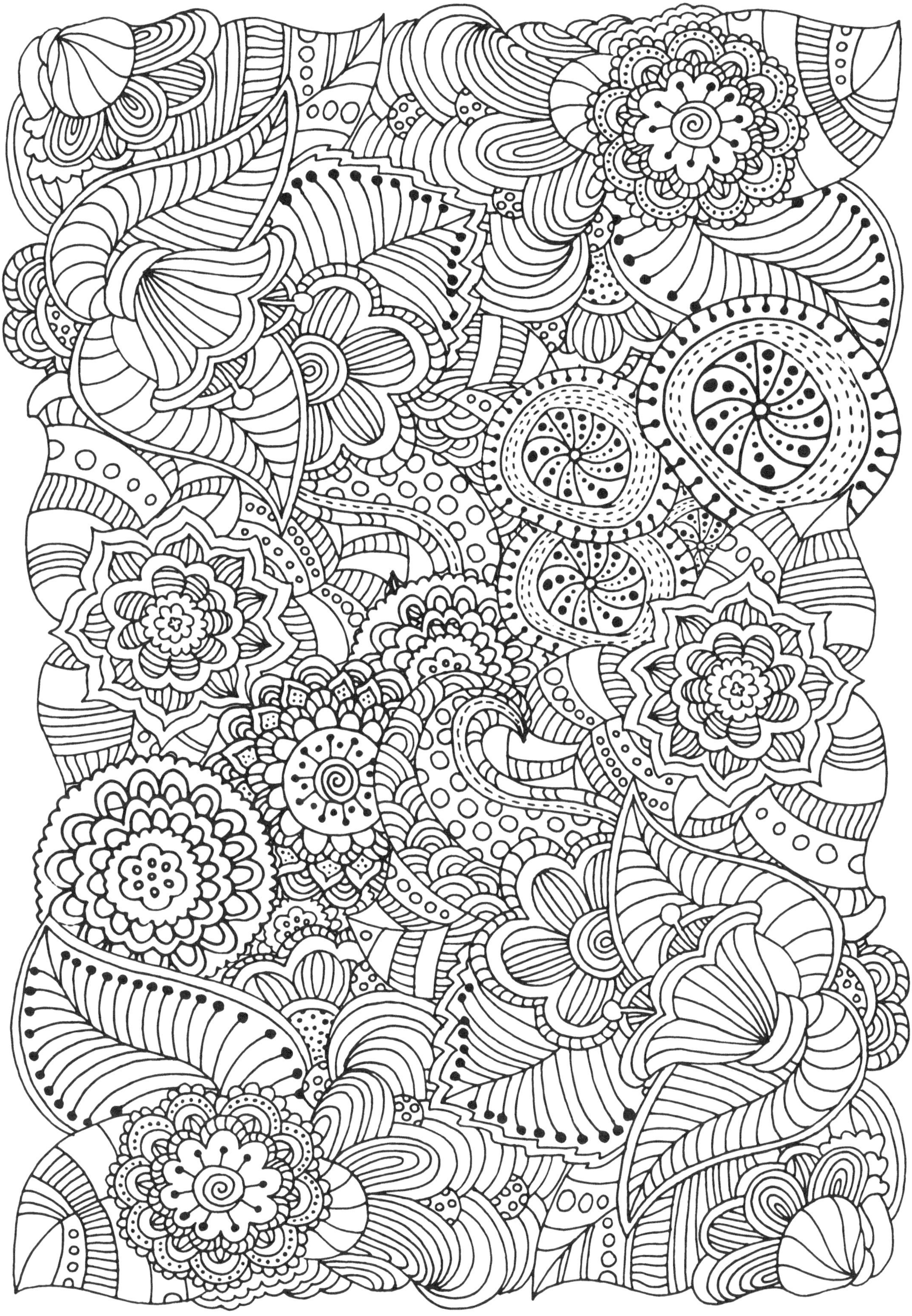

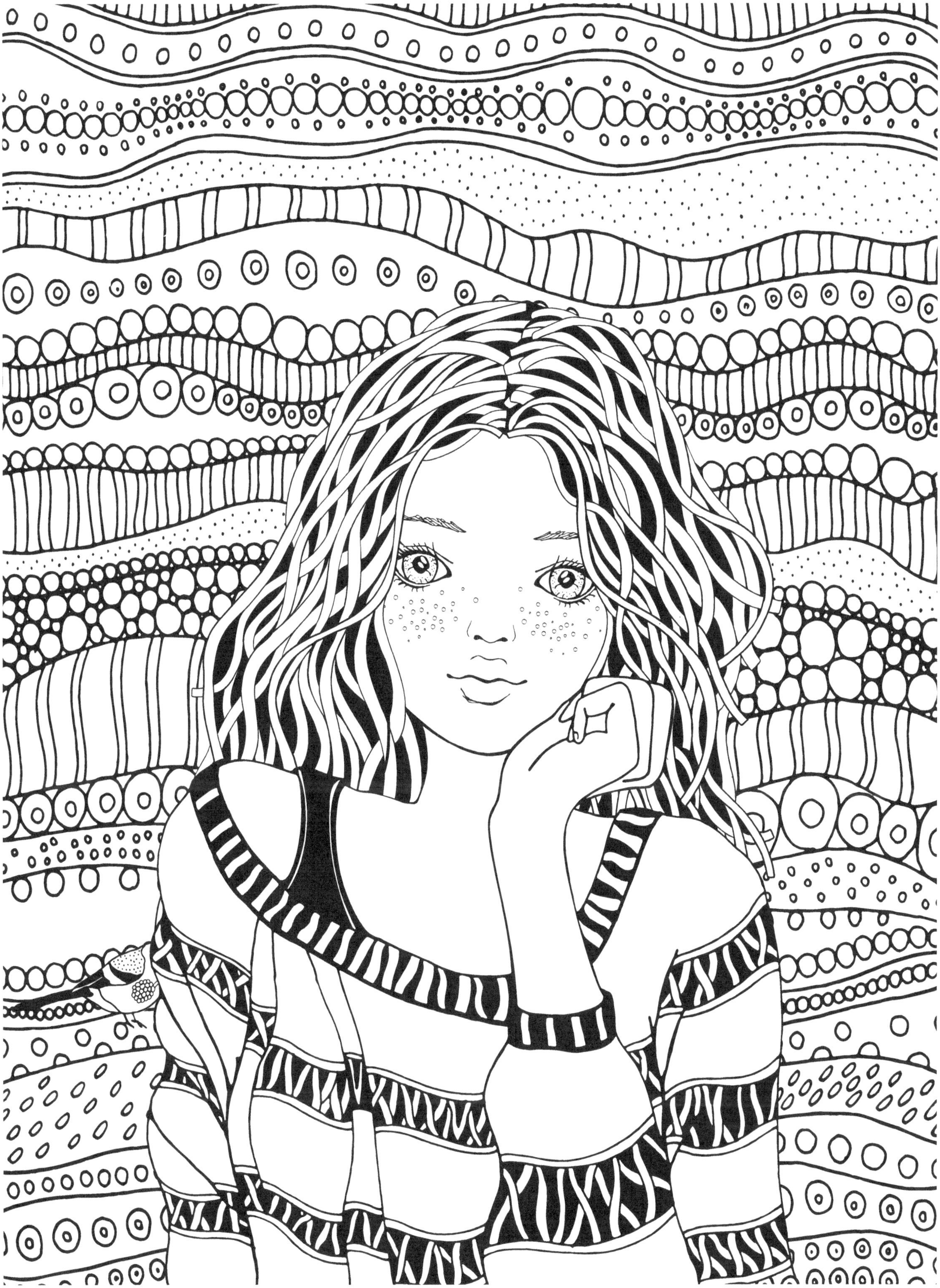

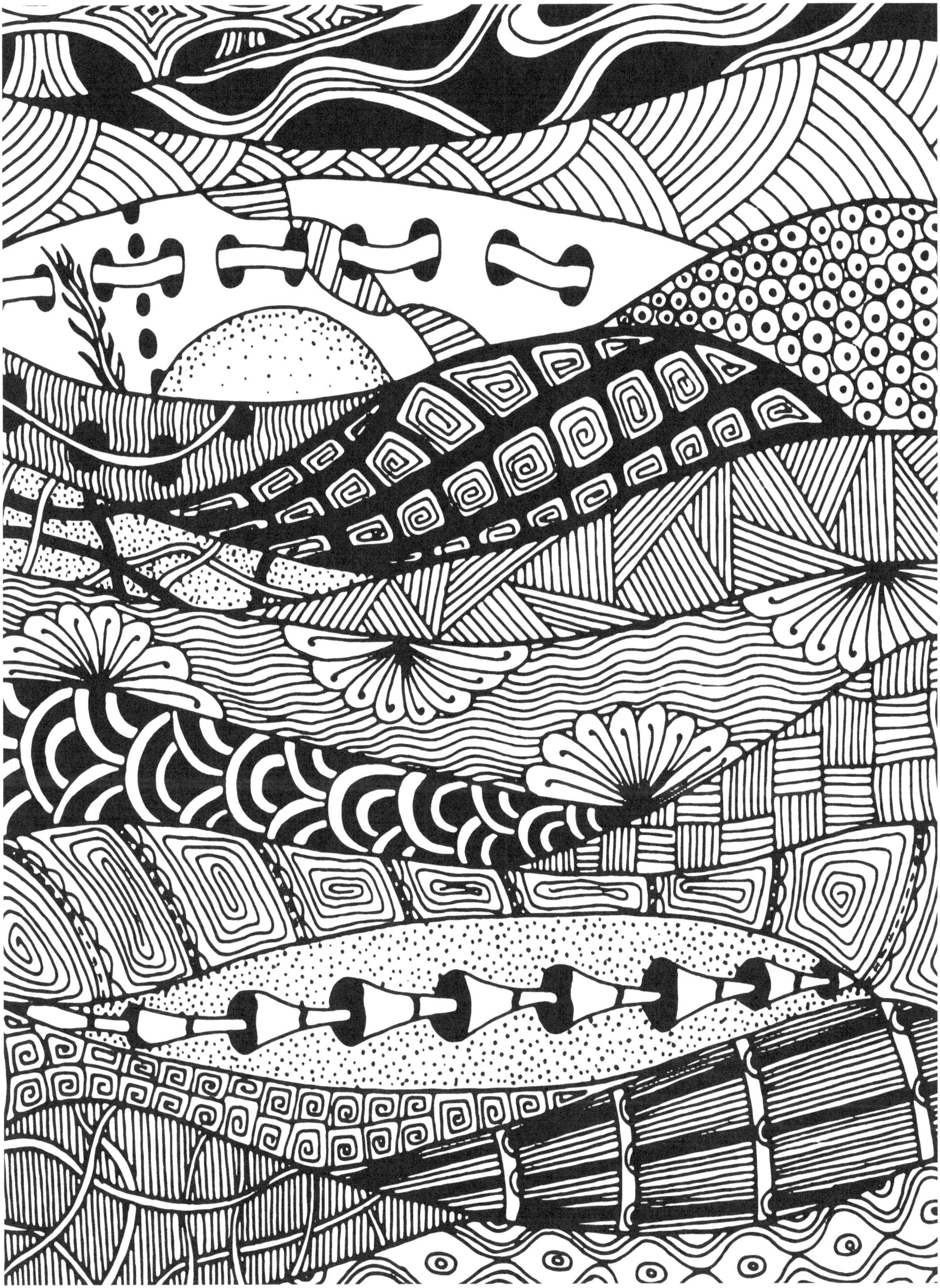

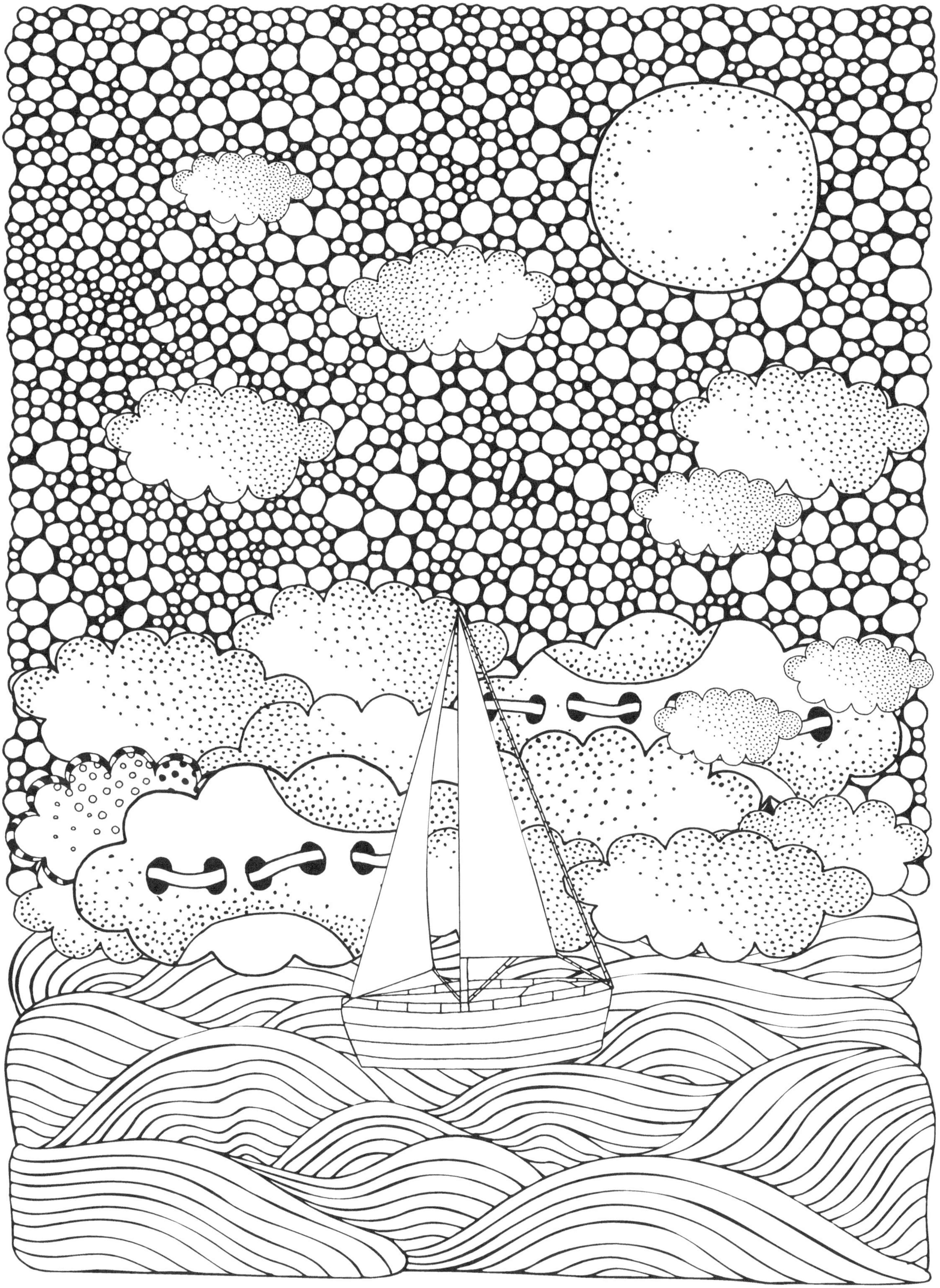

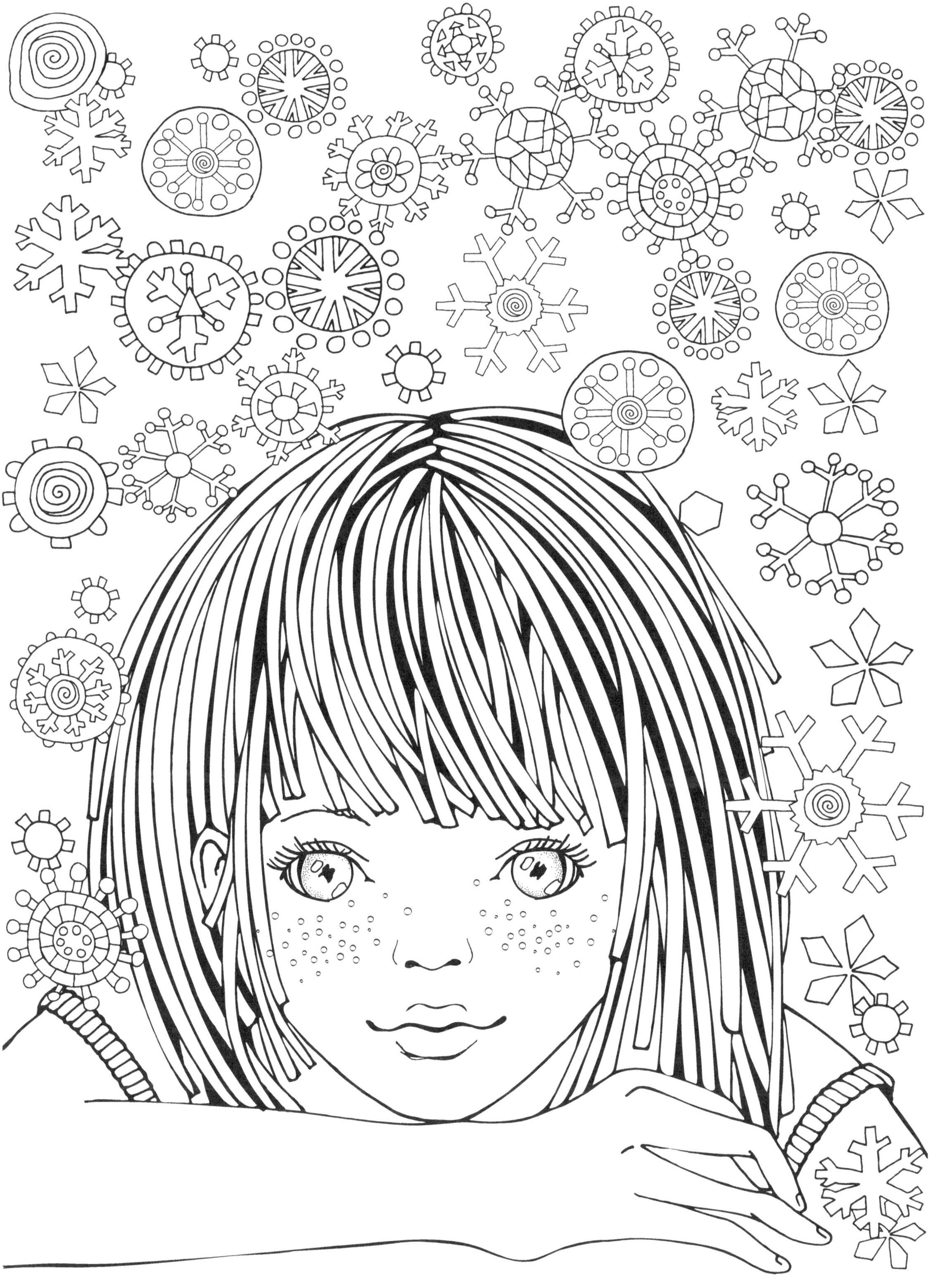

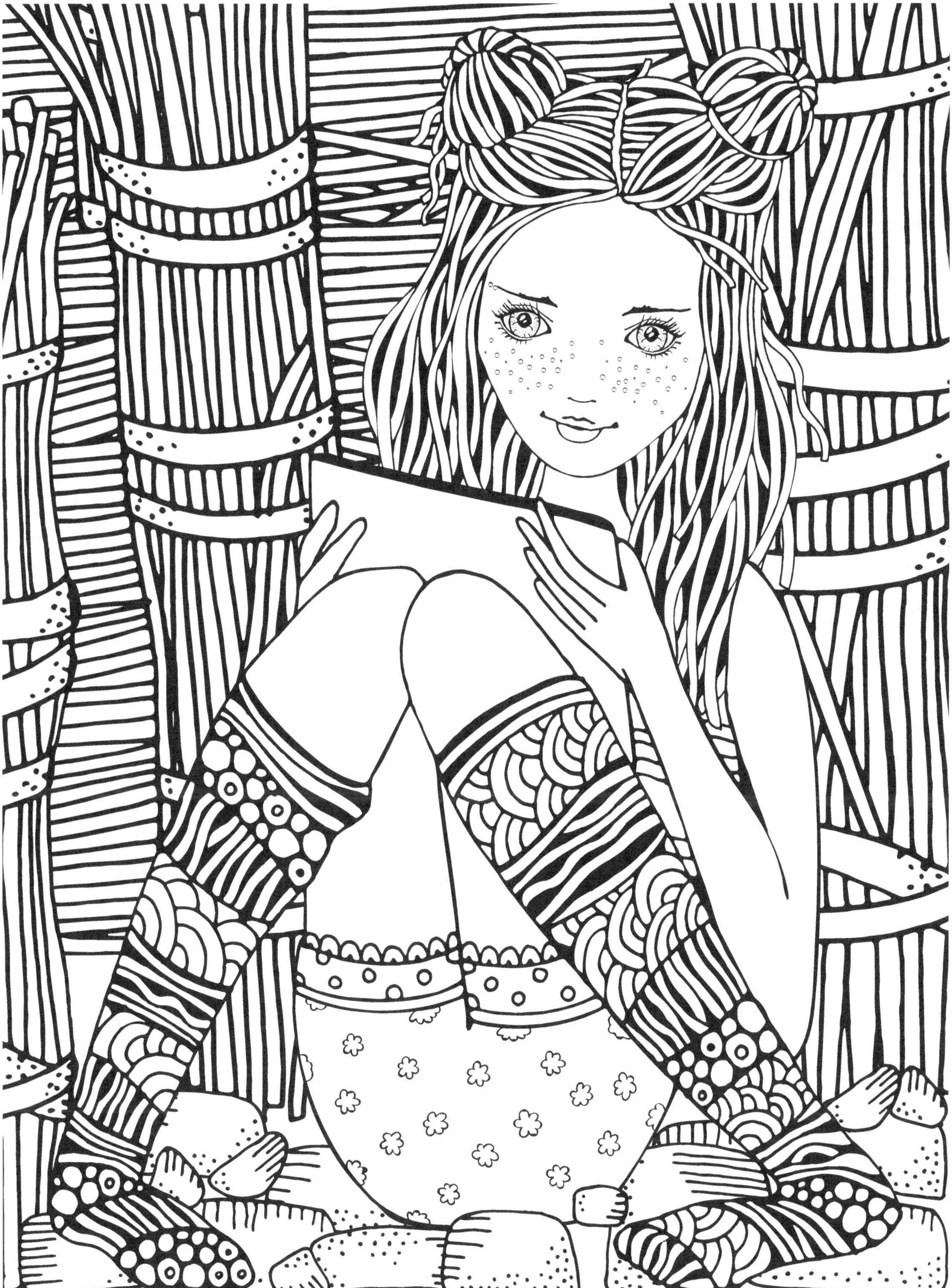

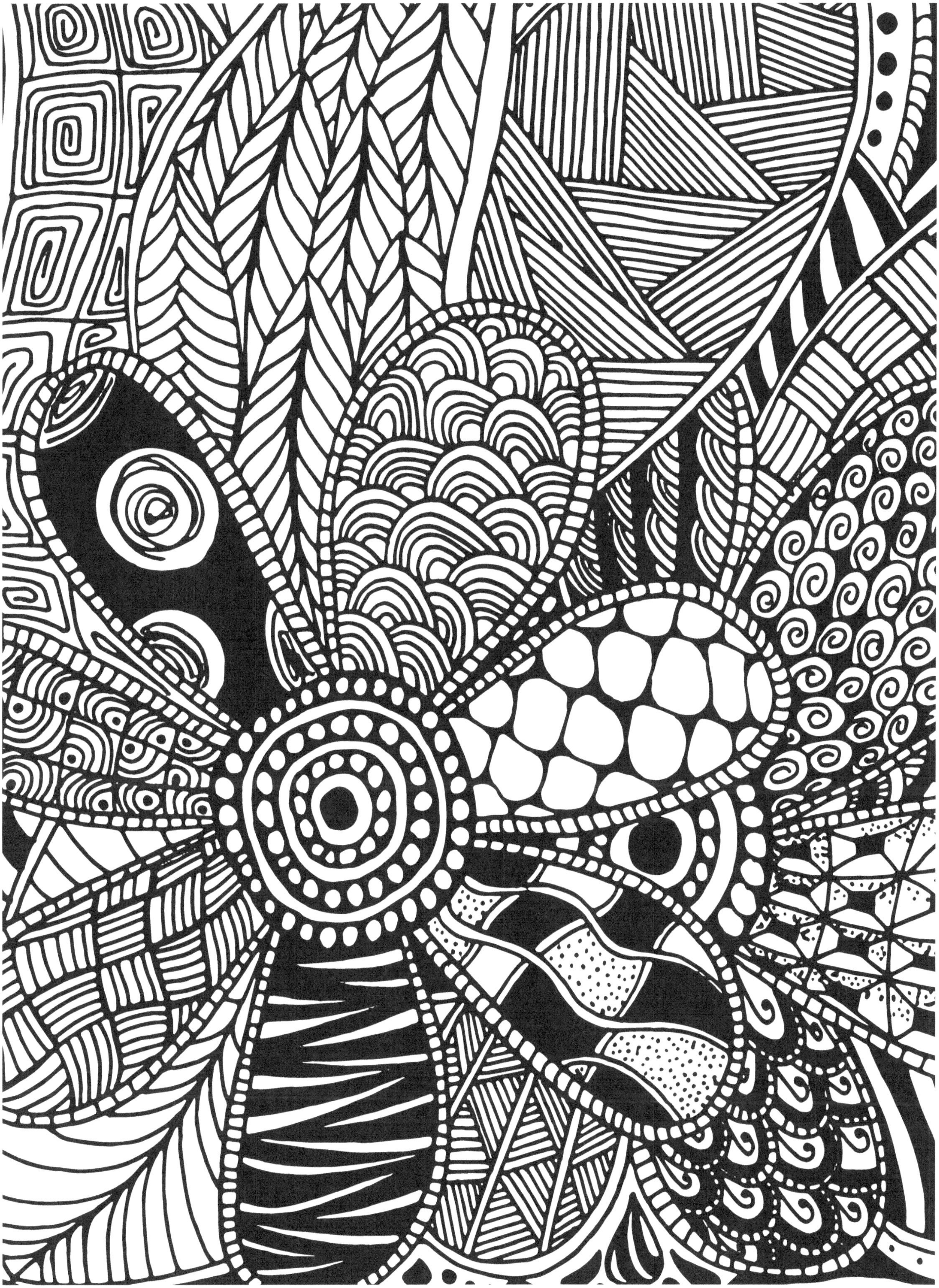

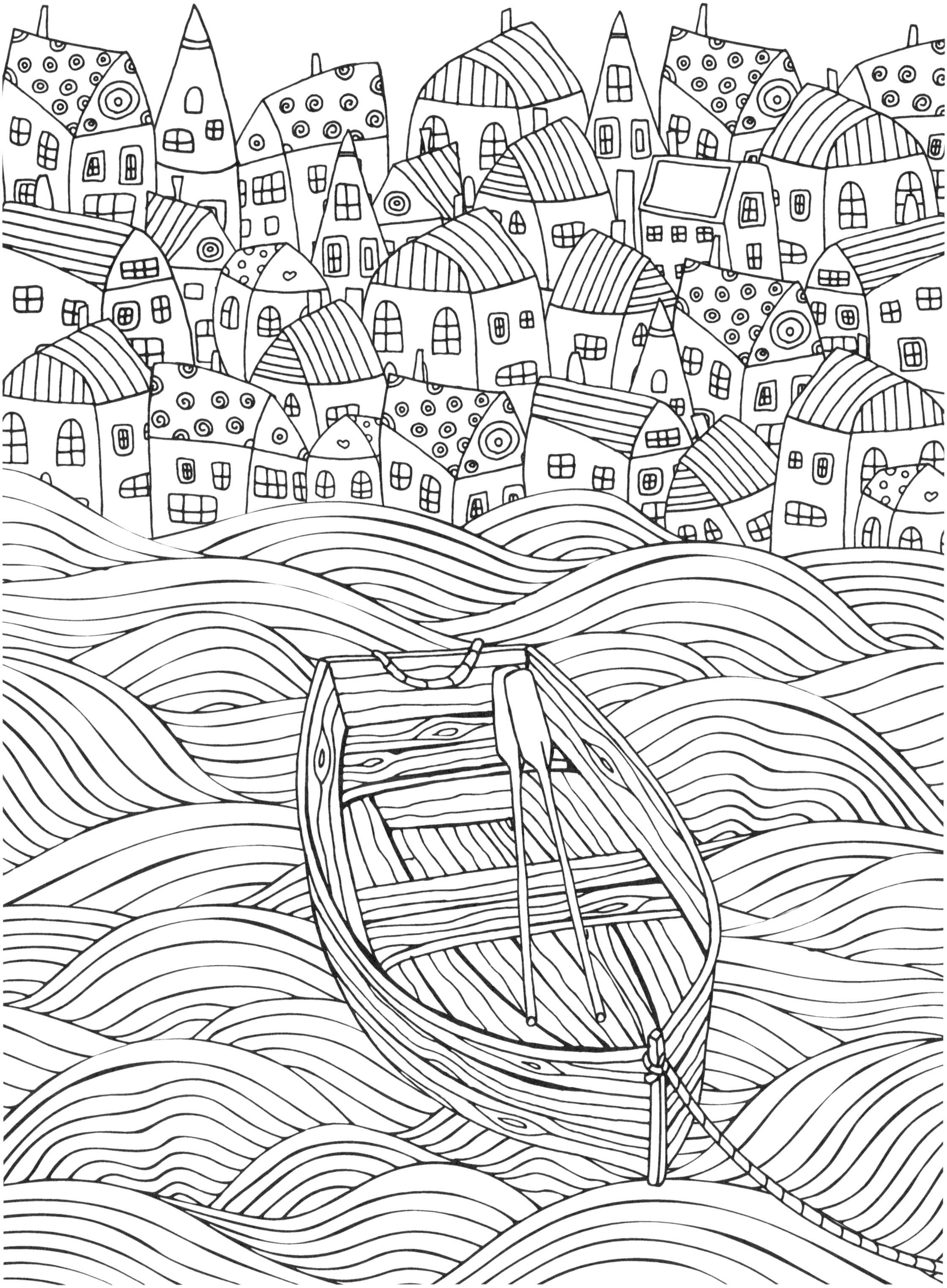

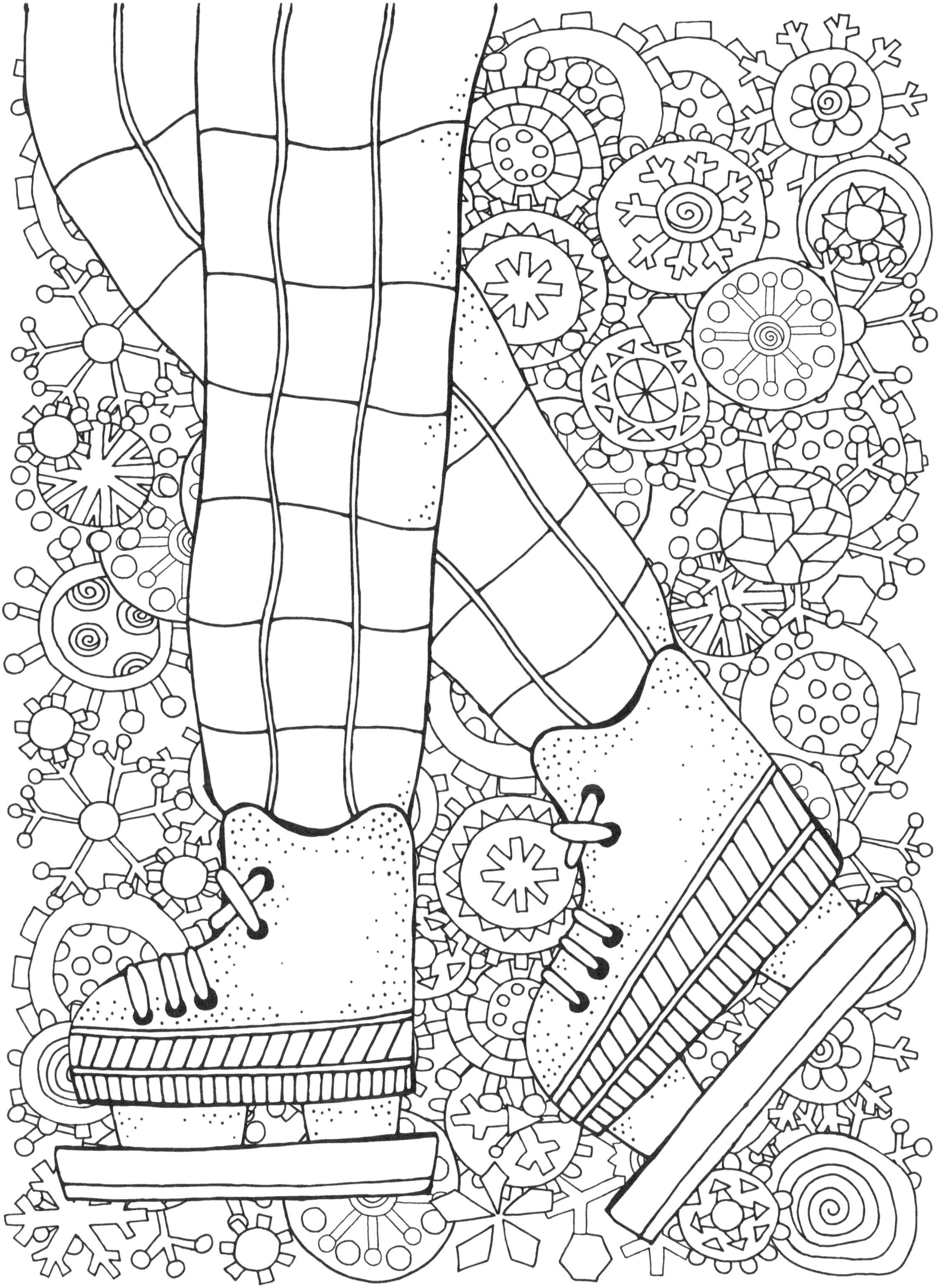

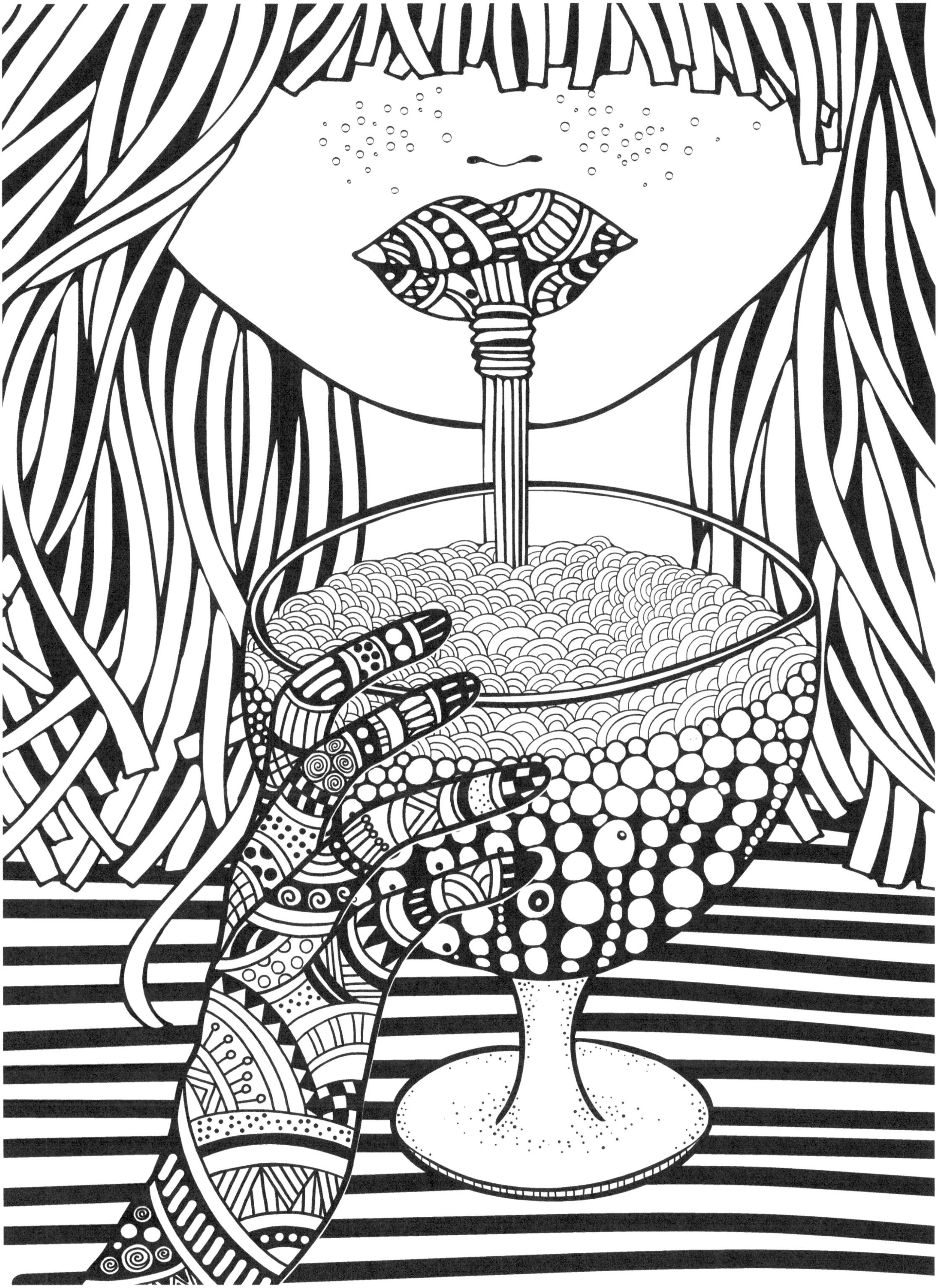

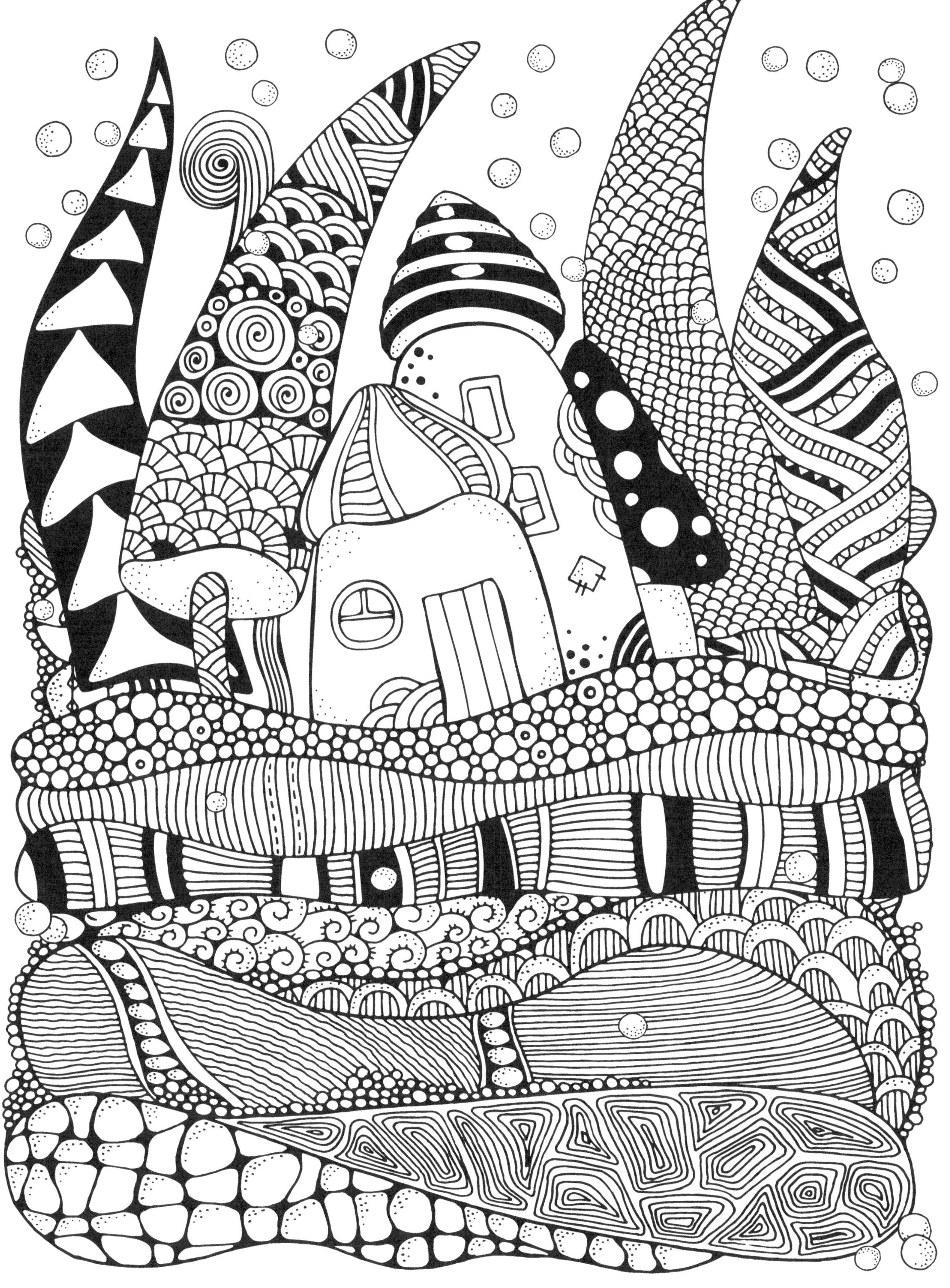

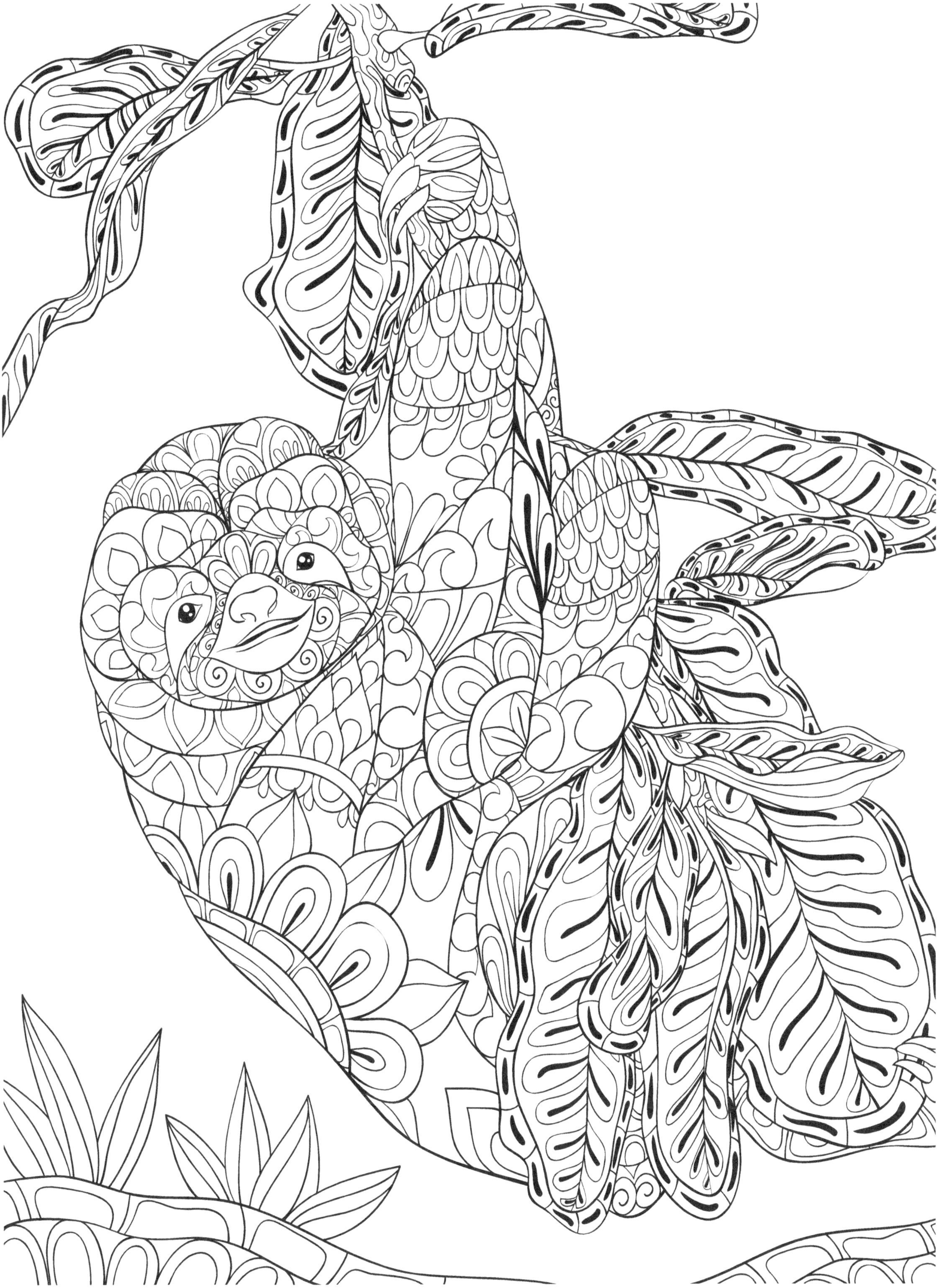

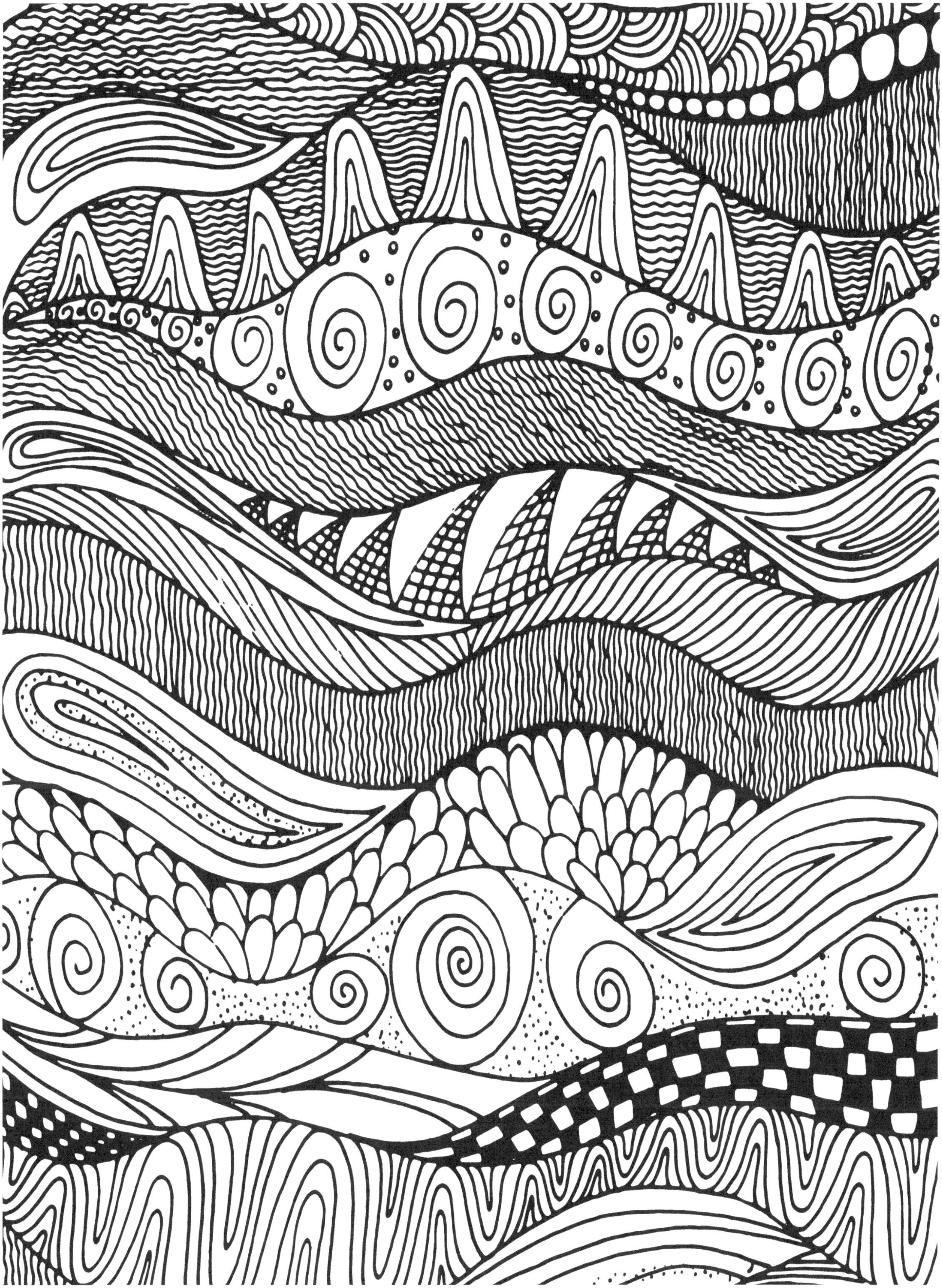

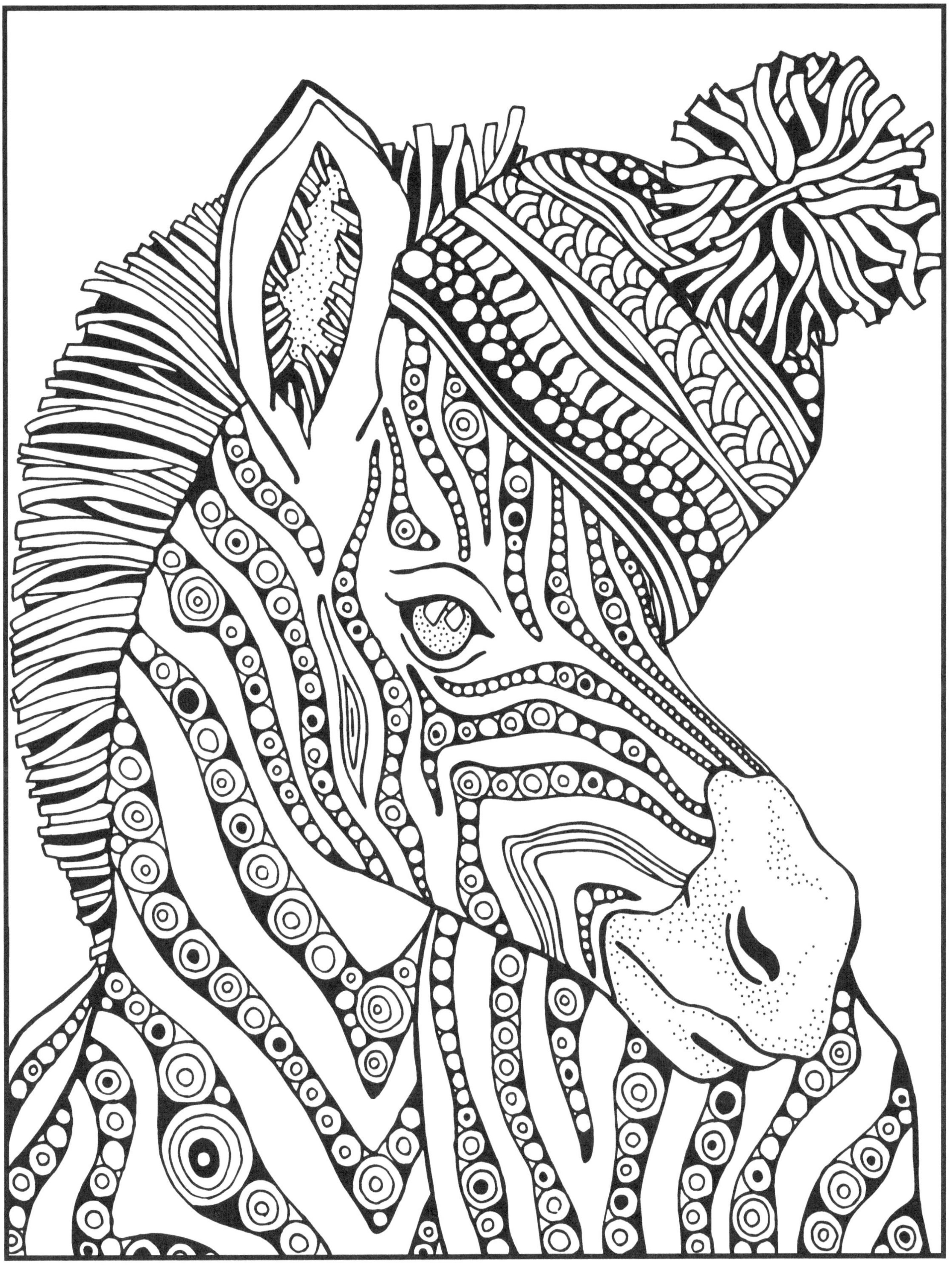

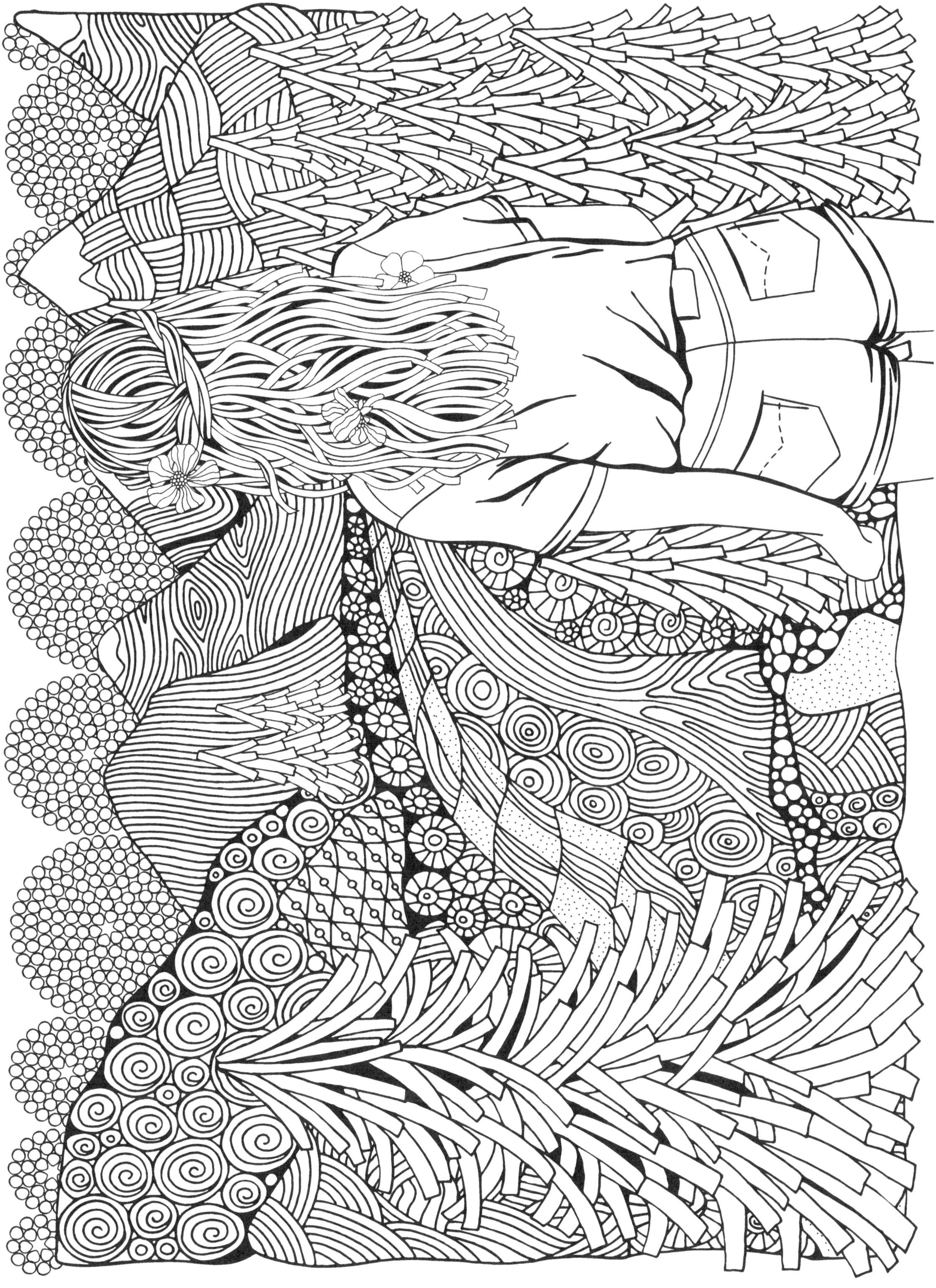

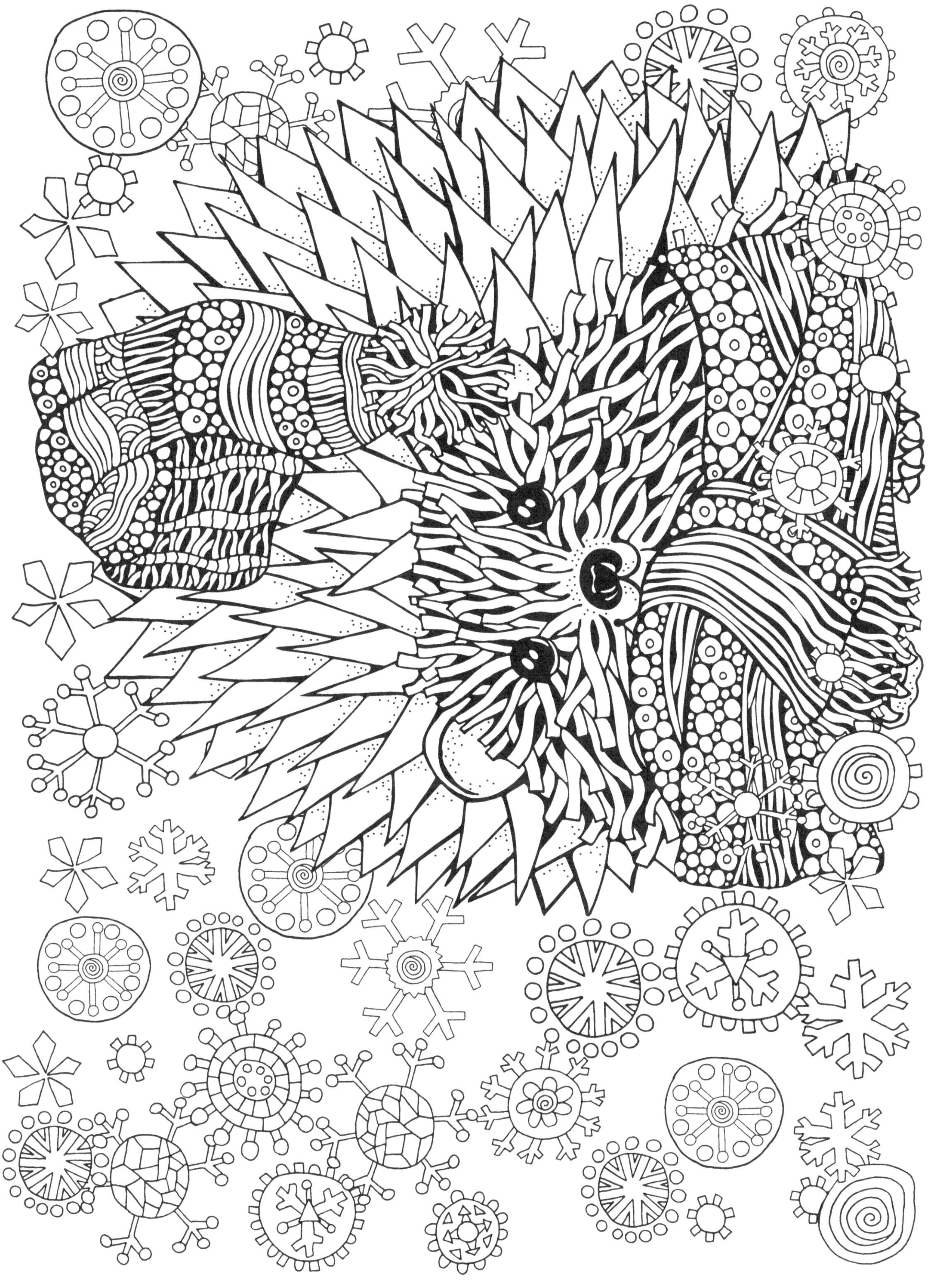

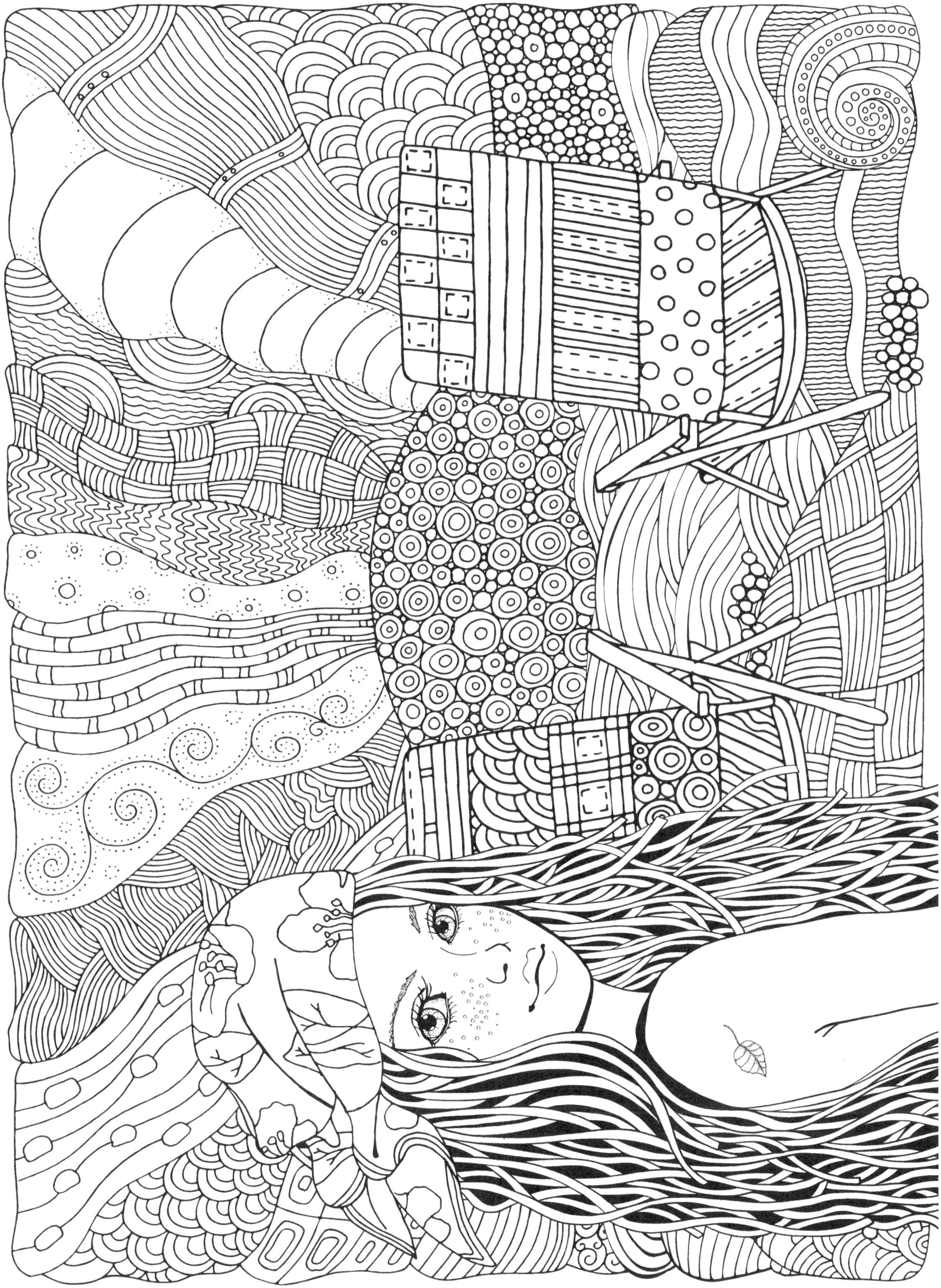

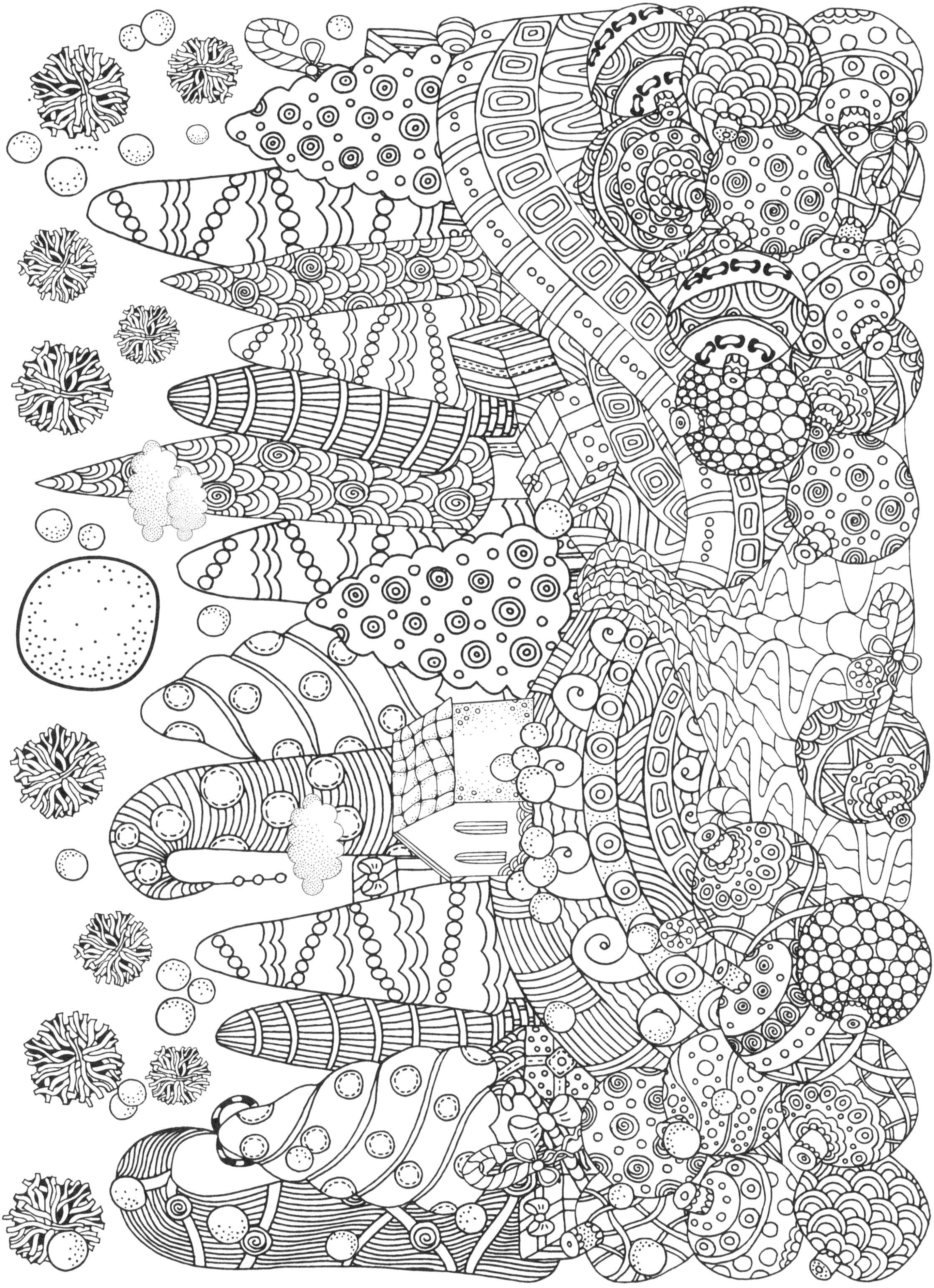

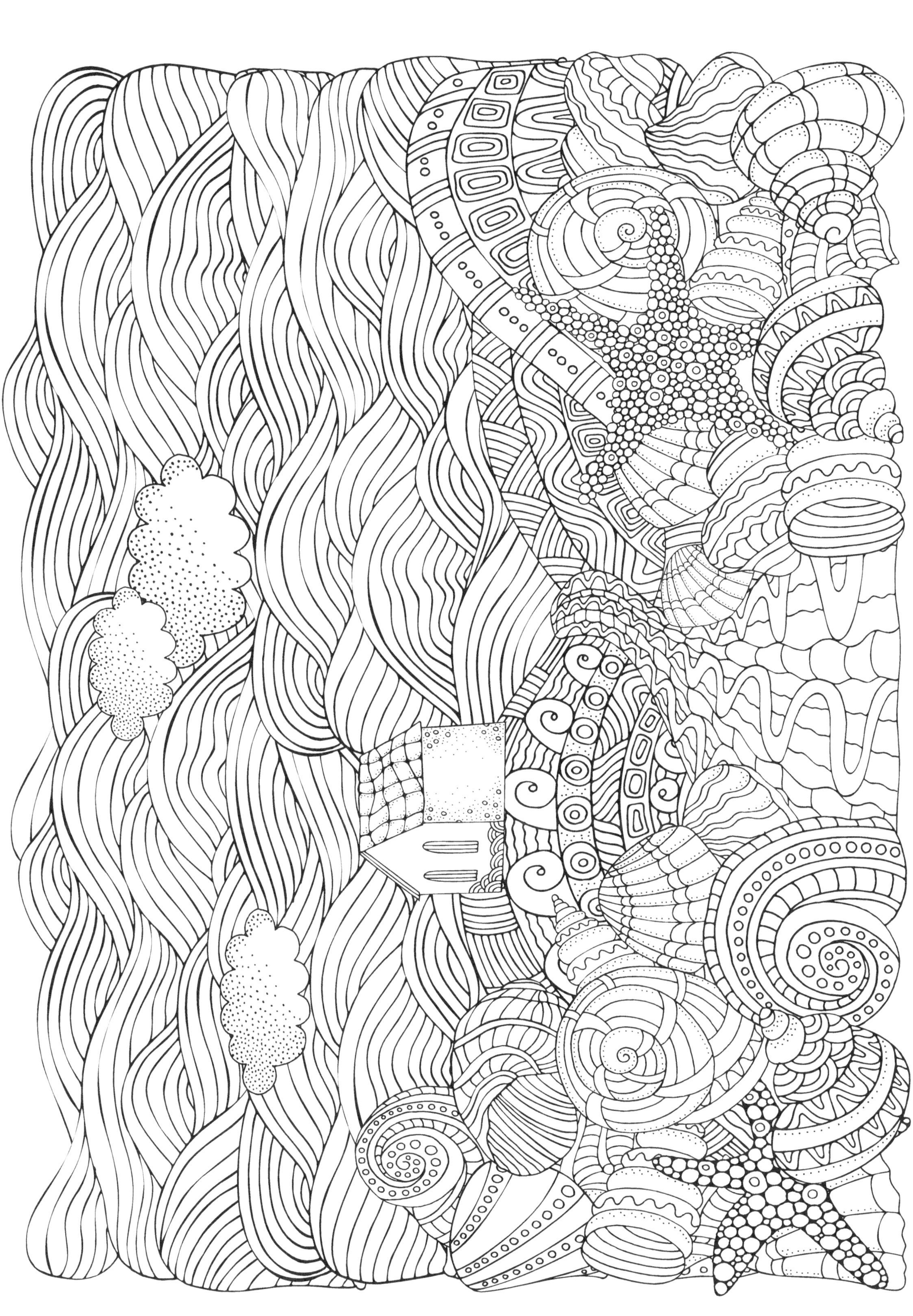

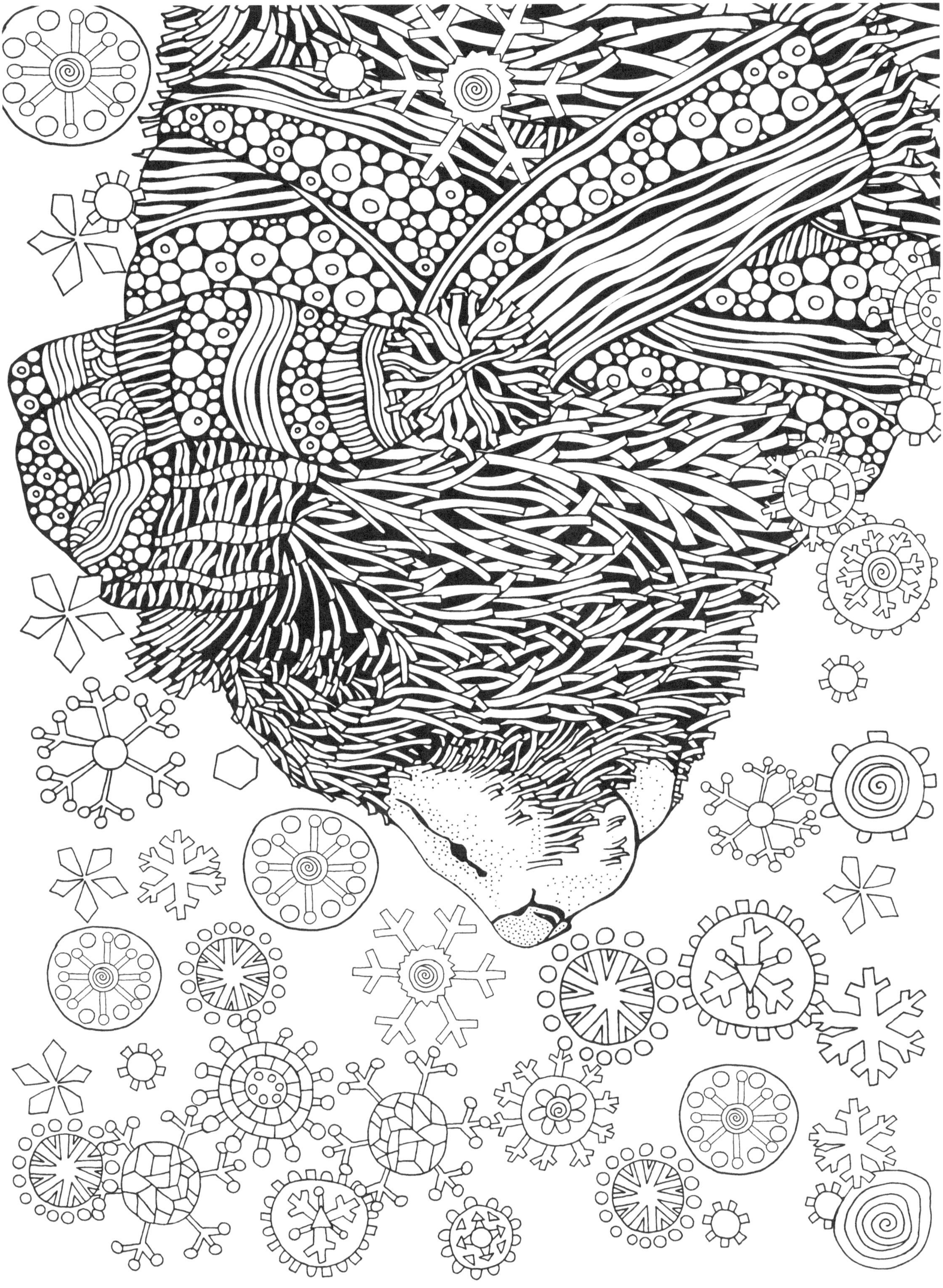

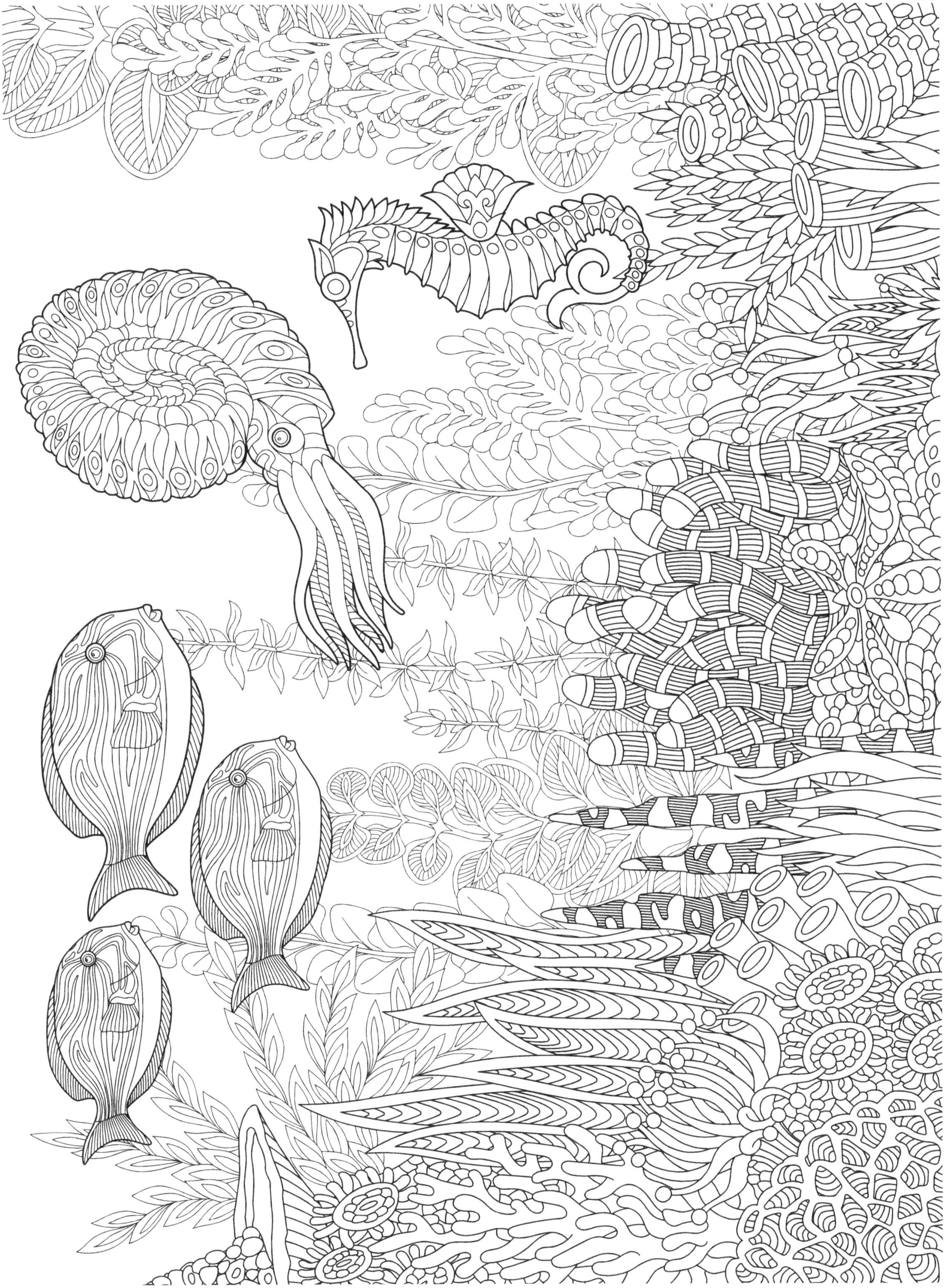

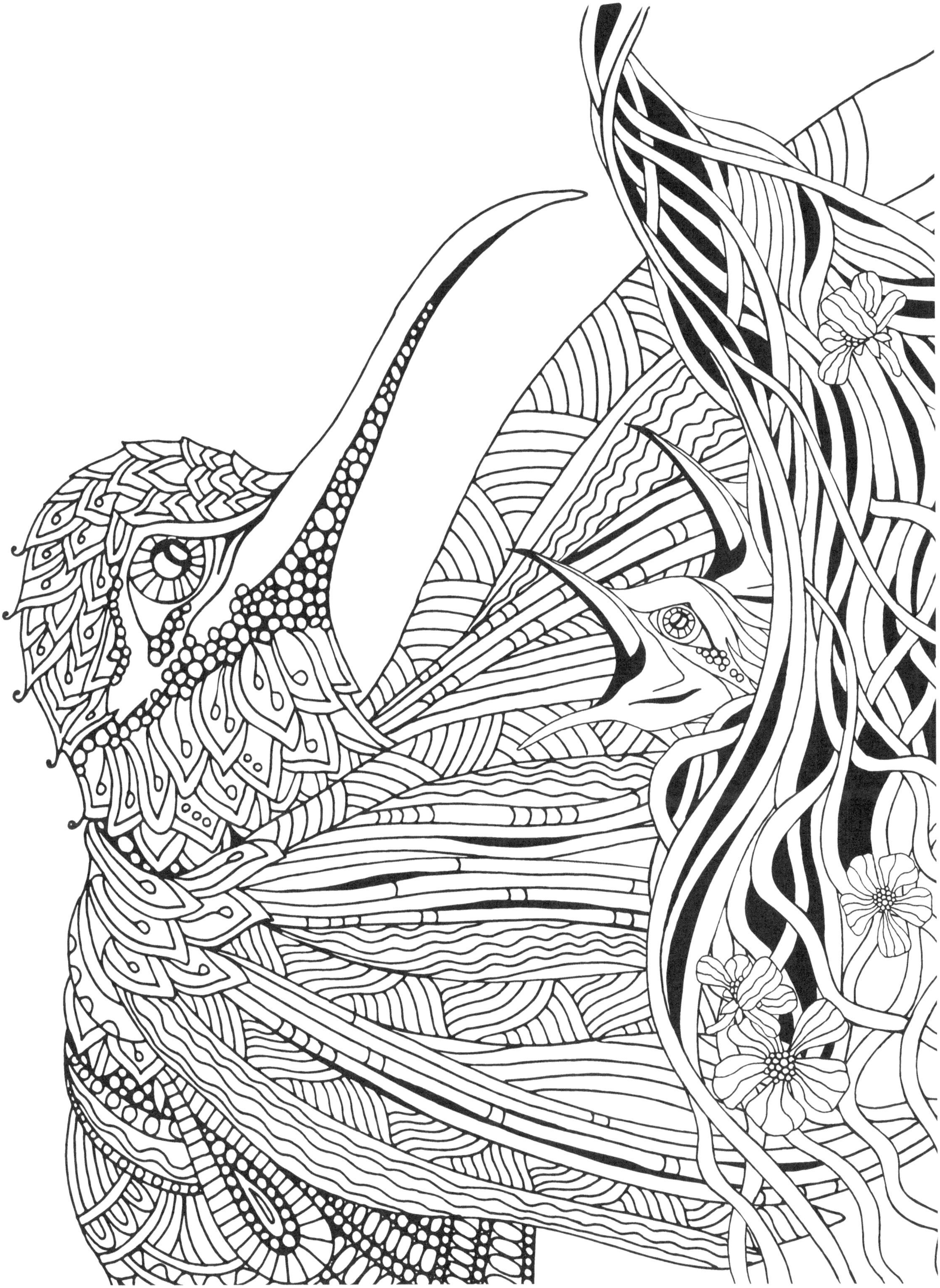

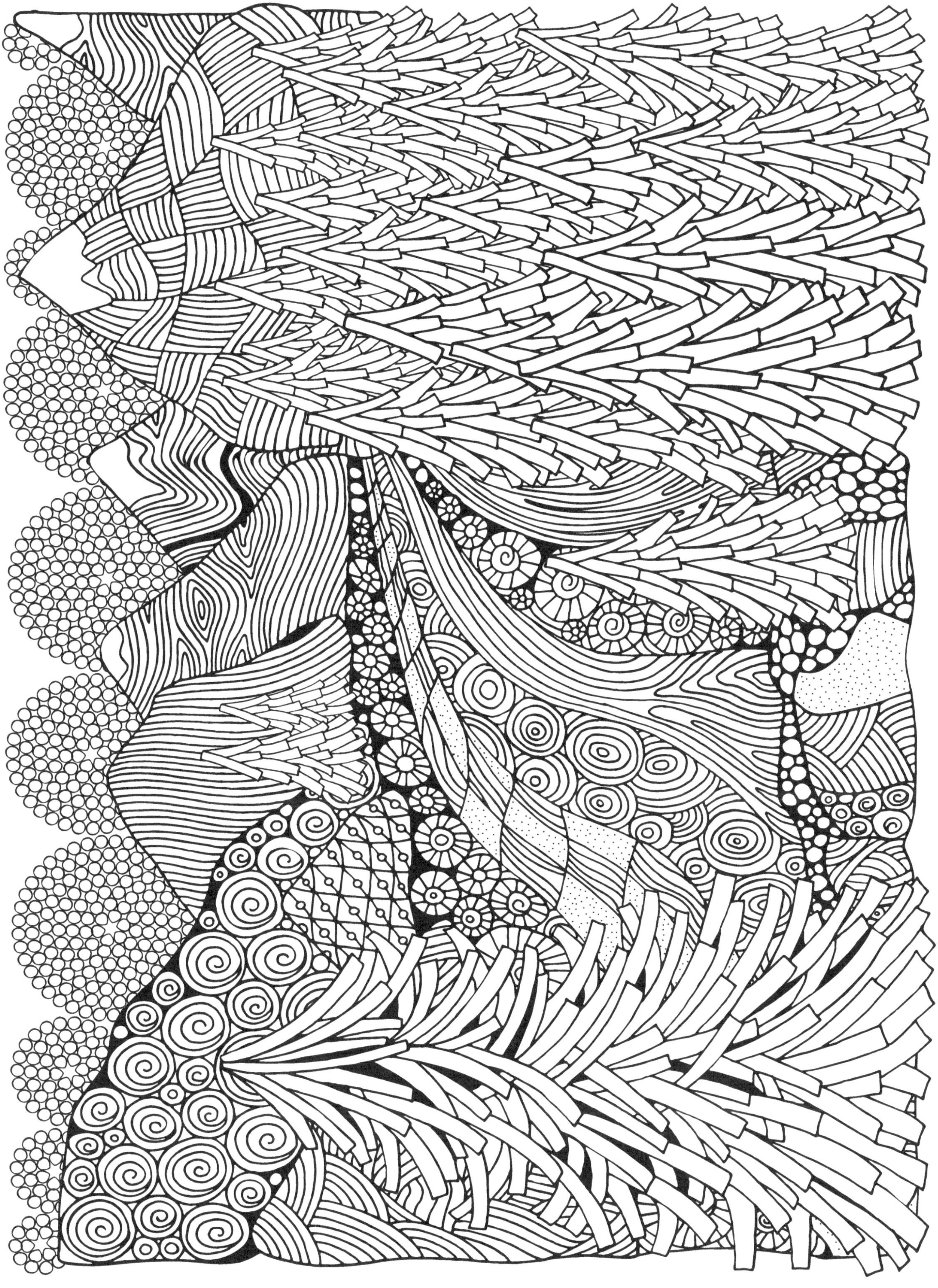

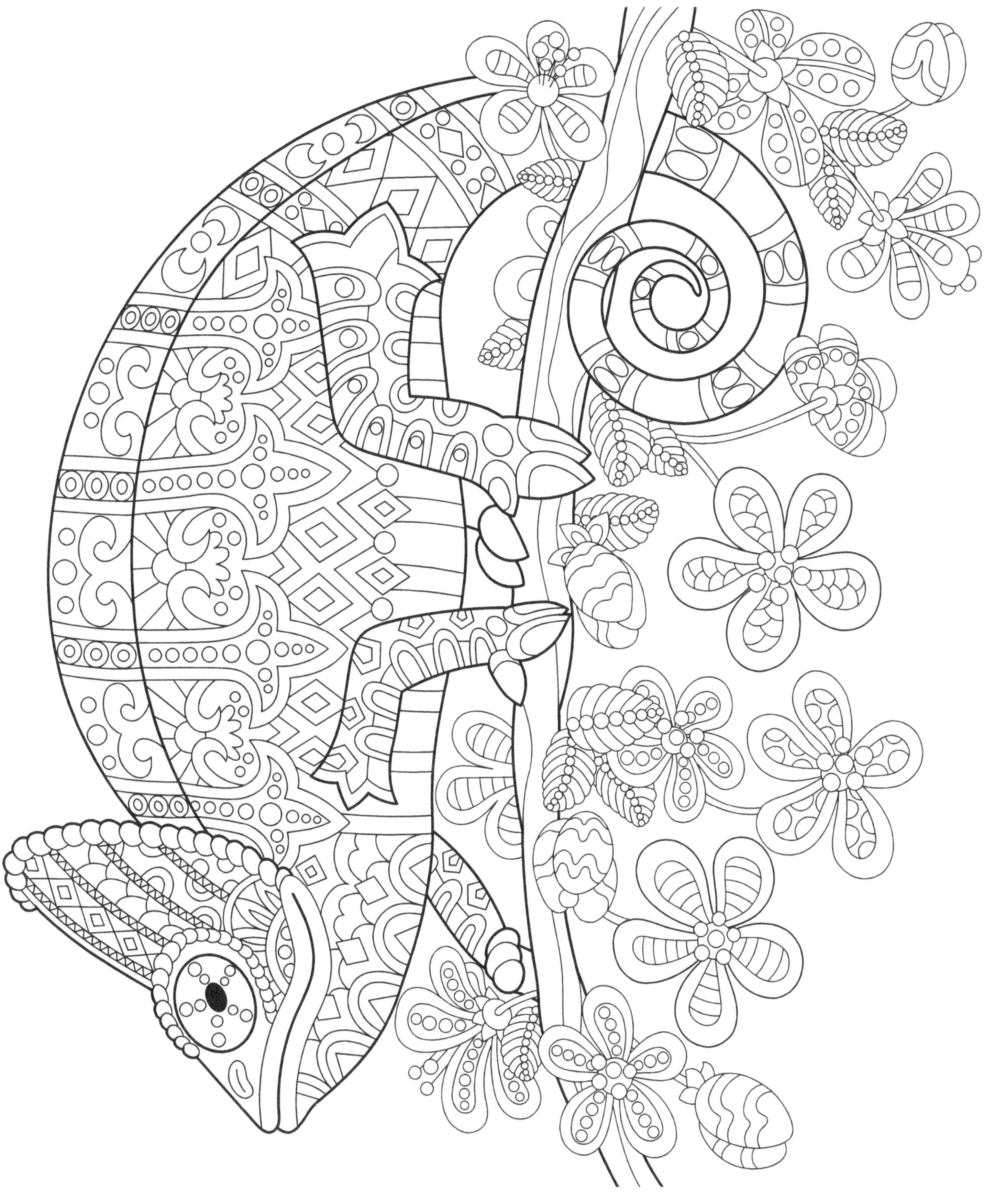

www.ingramcontent.com/pod-product-compliance
Lightning Source LLC
Chambersburg PA
CBHW082253220526
45469CB00009B/2992